# Using Market Research to Grow Your Business

■

Dear Pitman Publishing Customer

# IMPORTANT – Read This Now!

**We are delighted to announce a special free service for all of our customers.**

Simply complete this form and return it to the address overleaf to receive:

**A** Free Customer Newsletter

**B** Free Information Service

**C** Exclusive Customer Offers – which have included free software, videos and relevant products

**D** Opportunity to take part in product development sessions

**E** The chance for you to write about your own business experience and become one of our respected authors

Fill this in now and return it to us (no stamp needed in the UK) to join our customer information service.

Name:          Position:

Company/Organisation:

Address (including postcode):

Country:

Telephone:        Fax:

Nature of business:

Title of book purchased:

Comments:

- - - - - - - - - - - - - - - **Fold Here Then Staple** - - - - - - - - - - - - - - -

We would be very grateful if you could answer these questions to help us with market research.

**1 Where/How did you hear of this book?**

☐ in a bookshop

☐ in a magazine/newspaper
(please state which):

☐ information through the post

☐ recommendation from a colleague

☐ other (please state which):

**2 Which newspaper(s)/magazine(s) do you read regularly?:**

**3 When buying a business book which factors influence you most?**
(Please rank in order)

☐ recommendation from a colleague

☐ price

☐ content

☐ recommendation in a bookshop

☐ author

☐ publisher

☐ title

☐ other(s):

**4 Is this book a**

☐ personal purchase?

☐ company purchase?

**5 Would you be prepared to spend a few minutes talking to our customer services staff to help with product development? YES/NO**

# PITMAN PUBLISHING

*The Business Publisher*

Written for managers competing in today's tough business world, our books will help you get the edge on competitors by showing you how to:

- increase quality, efficiency and productivity throughout your organisation
- use both proven and innovative management techniques
- improve the management skills of you and your staff
- implement winning customer strategies

In short they provide concise, practical information that you can use every day to improve the success of your business.

**FINANCIAL TIMES**

**PITMAN PUBLISHING**

*in* the Institute of Management

*F O U N D A T I O N*

PITMAN PUBLISHING

---

Free Information Service
Pitman Professional Publishing
FREEPOST
128 Long Acre
LONDON
WC2E 9BR, UK

No stamp
necessary
in the UK

# Using Market Research to Grow Your Business

*How management obtain the information they need*

∎

ROBIN J. BIRN

the Institute of Management

FOUNDATION

PITMAN PUBLISHING

PITMAN PUBLISHING
128 Long Acre, London WC2E 9AN

A Division of Longman Group Limited

First published in Great Britain 1994

A CIP catalogue record for this book can be obtained
from the British Library

ISBN 0 273 60507 0

1 3 5 7 9 10 8 6 4 2

Photoset in Century Schoolbook by
Northern Phototypesetting Co. Ltd, Bolton
Printed and bound in Great Britain
by Bell and Bain Ltd, Glasgow

*The Publishers' policy is to use paper manufactured
from sustainable forests.*

*To Danit, Daniel and David*
*The Three 'Ds' who keep everything in perspective*

# Contents

∎

# Foreword

*by*
MICHAEL WARREN
*Director General, The Market Research Society*

■

One of my lasting memories of six years in the civil service was of a seminar, held one wet morning in an anonymous-looking building behind Victoria Station, on the collection and use of research in government. A senior civil servant (who had better remain nameless) was talking about his then Minister (who must definitely remain nameless).

'His views are quite simple and he has admitted them', said the civil servant. 'If research is going to support his case, it's a waste of money because he already knows what he's going to do. And if it's going to challenge his case, then it's also a waste of money because it's probably wrong. Besides which, he already knows what he's going to do.'

I found this deeply depressing. Survey research (or market research, or marketing research: there are a number of similar services with similar names) is a means by which the public's knowledge, needs, wants, concerns, doubts and plans – and even its behaviour – can be assessed. Indeed, for some sorts of data, research is not just a means, but *the* means. It's the only way of getting the information.

Surely government has a requirement – perhaps even a duty – to assess the population's cares and needs. It undoubtedly has a responsibility to take the decisions it believes to be right and necessary but isn't it better to take

difficult decisions knowing all – not just some – of the relevant background?

This is not simply a political point. The same is true of manufacturers or service providers. They have difficult choices to
make and, more often than not, need data on which to base
those decisions. The more data that is available, and the
higher its quality, the better.

This book will, I hope, encourage the developing use of survey research in industry's continuing search for the right
products, in the right markets, and at the right time and
price. Research can help in developing a product or service
(What do people need and want?), in the marketing of it (Is
the campaign comprehensible and persuasive?) and in
assessing its impact (Who is buying it, and do they like what
they've bought?).

In reading this book I was reminded of the systems in place
at another of my old employers – Consumers' Association,
publishers of *Which?* magazine. In the early 1980s, when I
worked there, survey research was seen as an essential part
of the process. It was one of the elements which had to be
taken account of, alongside, for example, data from the labo-
ratories (where the goods were tested), from the visits (to the
countries or resorts), from desk research, and, of course, from
CA's overall view of what was right.

Similarly, a manufacturer has a variety of pressures and
demands to cope with and – ultimately – to reconcile. There
is an inherent pressure from the firm's history and image,
there are the possibilities and limits of the firm's production
capacity, there are the skills of the sales force, there are leg-
islative constraints, and there are always, of course, the
accountants. And, increasingly often, there is research,

research to provide that key information about what the market wants and expects and does.

I have no doubt at all that the firm that has a well thought-out research programme in place is better equipped for the 1990s than one that doesn't, though I am aware – not least from my own professional life – that coping with increasing amounts of information is not always easy.

This book will, I trust, provide constructive and detailed ideas to firms that wish to join the growing band of organisations that have seen the value – perhaps even the necessity – of market research.

# Preface

*Information is all around us but how*
*many of us use it properly?*

■

*U*sing *Market Research to Grow Your Business* has been written to fulfill a number of objectives. Over the last 18 years of working in marketing and research I have been constantly interested in the fact that many managers take decisions without research. There are also many managers who do not recognise that research would help them to make better decisions.

I will never forget the situation I found myself in when I visited a company in the consumer durables sector, which is a leading brand in a sector which does not have any good marketing information; that is industry data to monitor market performance. I was visiting the company with a component supplier who was sponsoring us to work with the sector to set up a benchmark survey for this sector. We were making a presentation to the Managing Director who had recently been recruited from the fast moving consumer goods sector and who was used to using marketing information. In the meeting was his Sales Director, a man who had been working for the organisation for 35 years, without information.

Our proposition was to help the sector by developing a regular consumer survey to provide purchase and usership data to feed consumer purchase trends back to the manufacturer. The only data available to a manufacturer in this sector is based on the manufacturer's own sales figures to shops and independent market share data released by the shops. We presented the rationale of using data from the user and purchaser and how it would assist the company to achieve better sales and product planning. All the way through the presentation the Managing Director nodded in agreement with us and interjected comments of support and how he would make use of the information. The Sales Director kept silent.

We reached the point of showing a slide of how such information could be used by management, dividing it into actions by the sales people, actions by marketing and promotions and actions by product and research and development. The Sales Director looked at the slide, sat up in his chair with his face turning a purple that is consistent with the robes of an Archbishop, and started shouting at us. 'I know my customers, I know what they want. How can you tell me what they want as they talk to me as they have done for 35 years. You cannot really expect me to accept that giving me data from the consumer will give me more information than I get from our customers. Our customers know who their customers are and they tell us when they have problems. They call me up and we discuss the problems and within a very short time I have solved the problem so that the retailer can go back to his customer to re-assure him. You cannot seriously think that giving me consumer information is going to help me solve the consumer problems. What a waste of my time. I do not think you understand our business and how we work with our customers [the shop buyers and shop managers].'

The Managing Director was as startled as we were. He had felt that our presentation would assist the company in achieving the change that he felt was needed to get closer to the real buyer, the consumer who will decide on the product and use it.

The Sales Director started to shout again. 'I do not think we need to change. We have been having success with the customers and in the 35 years I have been working for the company we have always done things in the same way.' The Managing Director interjected saying, 'One of the problems of our market, which is linked to activity in the housing market, is that we are dependent on the economic cycle of boom and recession. What we need to do is to understand consumer needs more clearly, to identify how new products can stimulate buying activity and help smooth out the trend.' The Sales Director shouted again, 'You do not understand the market either. Our customers tell the consumer what he wants and therefore we have a clear understanding of his needs.'

I thought it was my turn to speak again and so I interjected, 'Well that is what we are talking about. We are suggesting that you participate in an industry survey which will evaluate consumer needs more clearly. You, as the survey sponsor, will have the data and you can use it in your presentations and sales meetings to your customers. This will, in turn, influence how the retailers communicate with the users and buyers, and provide both you and your customers with a better way of targeting consumers and satisfying their needs.' The Sales Director started shouting again. 'That's not the way we do it in this business. Our customers tell us if there is a problem and we solve it. Our customers are not going to be interested in any information on their customers.'

It was at this point that the Managing Director, who had become very embarrassed about the whole situation got angry and suggested that we conclude the meeting. He decided to show us to the reception and we courteously said farewell to the over confident and now 'over hot' Sales Director. The Managing Director impressed on us how appreciative he was that we came and that he would be grateful if all the communications in future were only with him.

A few weeks later we received a telephone call from the Managing Director. He asked about how we were progressing with getting his competitors to provide support for this industry survey. We informed him that the other three leading companies in the sector had expressed an interest and it would be possible to develop the project. Support from his company was also important. He said that he wanted to join the Research Group and that he would get back to us to confirm this once he had agreed the areas with his *new* Sales Director, as he had advised the old Sales Director to find a new life in retirement. As a result, the company became one of the sponsors to the project.

This situation and many similar situations indicate that the role, and to some extent the image, of market research is not clear, strong and focused as an important management tool. Market researchers of course believe that market research is important, but they have not been as successful as the advertisers in communicating to management how they need to depend on it. The 1990s will see a change in the image of market research from being the area of the technician to becoming the realm of the problem solver and adviser.

This change is important for any company because of the volume and extent of information. And what is also going to be a characteristic is that more senior management will become information-dependent as the ability to collect information is further simplified through additional technological development. With markets becoming more competitive, senior management is going to demand more proof of the opportunities or niches to develop than they have been doing in the past.

So I felt it was important to demonstrate how fundamental marketing research is to the sales and marketing process. It is also interesting to demonstrate the importance and relevance of marketing research to all levels of management, because if designed correctly, it can be used effectively. Marketing research can also provide management with a better insight into making research work and assist in the company and its success.

This book clarifies the essential techniques of market research that management needs to know. It explains why research is needed, what it is and how companies which have not used it much in the past become dependant on it. It clearly shows how market research helps to plan, focus and drive the marketing process, and provide the necessary independent feedback on whether management is making the right or wrong decisions. It also shows the difference between good and bad ways of doing market research and the implications of not taking it on board effectively.

*Using Market Research to Grow Your Business* has to be both useful and important to management. Marketing is all about satisfying customers. Research is all about getting the best feedback to ensure that customers are satisfied. A company which knows its customers and monitors its activity well, and has a good understanding of the key research techniques it needs, is likely to develop better and more competitive sales, marketing and communications strategies.

A company will grow its business if it is better equipped to approach its market in the knowledge of customer needs, having confirmed what they like and dislike and targeting its products and services more specifically.

Robin Birn
Strategy, Research & Action
Parkway House
Sheen Lane
London
SW14 8LS

# Acknowledgements

■

*'We are such stuff as dreams are made of and our
little lives are rounded with a sleep'*
WILLIAM SHAKESPEARE
*The Tempest*

Dreams can only be fulfilled if those who experience them, or even 'appear' in them, take decisions that cause them to replicate the ideas, thoughts and situations in reality. Many feel that their lives are more meaningful if their sleep is interrupted or, as some say, made more interesting with a dream in the middle. Whatever the experience of a person with a dream, it stands as an example which can be followed or, for those who have unpleasant ones, avoided. Managers are always interested in fulfilling dreams because they are eager to follow examples demonstrated in case studies. It is the way in which they believe they can become more creative in their decision making, taking the example of others to achieve the dreams they want to achieve for their own companies.

Authors are also dependent on experiences to make their books the dreams that can be achieved by the reader. However, when writing business books, the authors are more likely to relate with experiences shared with colleagues, friends and companies with whom work has been completed. It is only through the media of written communications that an opportunity to express true appreciation for the interest and support that is realised in such a project as this can be expressed with the gratitude it deserves. I therefore want to be able to say how I appreciate the opportunities we have had, particularly in the last ten years, when some of what follows in this book has been realised and developed by those we have had the pleasure to work with.

Specific appreciation must be expressed too to a number of people who have been involved in some form or other that has given me the time, resource and support to write this book. I want to thank my family for their support in giving me time to write the book, sometimes early in the morning, sometimes late at night. They have also been tremendous with expressing their further support for the heavy international travelling schedule that has become part of the working life over the last two years. This schedule also gave me time to write parts of the book at 35,000 feet with the world's favourite airline looking after me, with those passengers sitting next to me irritated that they could not talk because I was busy writing a chapter.

Others have also been involved in helping to review how research can grow business in the working environment and they also deserve thanks for their involvement. Derrick Mitchell of Naturin GmbH, Wienheim, Germany, has been interested in the application of a series of the ideas in the book, particularly the 'win-win' theory. Mike Cranidge, Ordnance Survey, Southampton, and other members of the UK Map, Atlas and Travel Guide Research Group for working hard to implement research effectively. Mike McDermott, US Geological Survey, Reston, Virginia, for helping me to make the dreams of using my US/UK dual nationality to its ultimate effect and becoming involved in global marketing, rather than just talking about it. Patrick Forsyth, Touchstone Training & Consultancy, London, for giving me the opportunity of developing the courses in the Asia-Pacific Region, which have tested out some of the chapters that follow in interactive sessions with delegates. David Senton, Touchstone Training & Consultancy, for reviewing the last chapter and adding some key points of interest to managers. Michael Warren, Market Research Society, London, and Lorraine Hinchliffe, Market Research Society, for their interest and support, together with all of the MRS council and secretariat. Sue Garner, Strategy, Research & Action, London, for word processing and transcript and spotting errors in the sequence of the argument. My father for my US nationality and creating the index for the book.

Pitmans are also a team to be thanked for including *Using Market Research to Grow Your Business* in the Institute of Management series, as there are few titles which are non-technical and which are written to help management understand and use the techniques of research effectively.


Robin Birn

# Introduction

∎

**M**arket research is a management technique on which many people have different views – is it right or wrong, effective or useful? Few managers know how to do it well, realise how it can contribute to decision making and how it can be used to monitor whether these decisions are providing continued success.

Many managers think that research is only required if there is a problem to solve, if there are internal issues to answer or if a consensus view needs to be reached. Management can also mistake the usefulness of research as a picture of a situation, a 'snap shot' or answer to a problem, thinking that once information is collected it represents the view of the market or customer for all situations and all times. That situation cannot be true for anyone who understands marketing, as customers' needs and market situations are always changing. Research thus has the role of analysing these changes, identifying routes to success and monitoring whether decisions are effective.

There is a difference between market research – identifying the size, shape and nature of markets and marketing research – evaluating which sales, marketing and communications methods are accepted, liked and effective in a market. The former is the traditional use of research techniques, the latter is an emerging trend for companies to establish whether they are getting their marketing decisions right or wrong in relation to competitors. It is also the more successful way in relating how research helps to grow business.

The boom of the 1980s saw more companies using marketing research to develop their ideas, creative approaches and techniques for attacking market segments. The benefits of the research techniques were therefore appreciated and used by more levels of management, affecting company culture in the ways in which decisions were taken based on data and objective information.

The recession of the early 1990s has seen not only a further development of the use of marketing research, but companies have started to recognise the essential role of using information to decide on how to allocate resources cost effectively and monitor the return on the investments made. What is still uncertain is the realisation that research itself is only cost effective if it is completed on a continuing basis, to monitor the results of decisions taken, assess competitors' reactions and identify also the changing needs of customers.

*Using Market Research to Grow Your Business* has been written to focus management thinking on how carefully designed research can enable management make the right decisions, develop products and services that are 'user friendly' and set marketing and promotional budgets which are precisely spent and provide measurable returns. I have included examples of companies that have said they use research in this context. The interesting aspect of these case studies is that they show the decisions that have been taken as a result of the research, which are convincing in themselves as they say that monitoring their markets has been helpful to them.

## Defining market and marketing research

Most market research books start with the traditional

definitions of market research developed by the Chartered
Institute of Marketing, the American Marketing Association
or the Market Research Society of Great Britain. There is
nothing wrong with these definitions, but they are precise
and descriptive of the positioning of research techniques in
the marketing process.

I want to produce definitions that are more relevant to the
use of research or illustrate the reasons why it should be
used. Let us look at my 'working' definition and establish its
relevance to your organisation.

3

**Figure 1  Research definition**

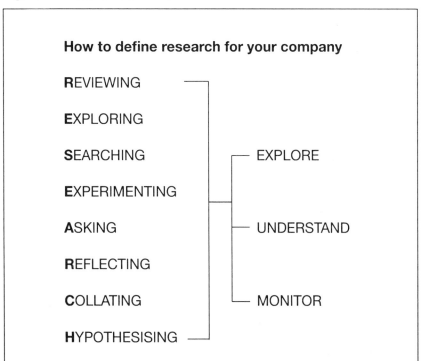

# Reviewing what is needed by the company

The initial task for management is to review what information exists in the company and whether 'information gaps' are causing the company to take decisions without obtaining the appropriate feedback from the market. The review should not be in the context of what the company can afford, but what is essential in reducing the uncertainty of taking decisions. Investing in collecting data therefore has to be a process which a manager needs to be committed to and recognises that it can improve the methods of working and taking important strategic and tactical decisions. A useful way of completing this phase is to list out all the facts that all managers in the company agree they do know as well as those they do not know. This provides a definitive list of information that can be collected.

Establishing the nature of information that is required through a detailed review should be exhaustive. Identifying what is required, when it is required and how it should be used will not only establish the priorities for how the data should be collected, but also aspects of the detail needed.

An exhaustive review will have a direct effect on the nature of the research that is carried out. It is likely to be better prepared, better designed and relate more specifically to the requirements of the company, its positioning in the market and the relative activities of competitors. The research is therefore going to be more useful as a result.

# Exploring what data exists

The exploration process is the key to agreeing what research is required in the short, medium and long term. Many managers do not realise that they either have good information that is not being used, or that they have invested in computer systems which can help them to collate and analyse good data if they were confident in using it.

Internally, financial accounts information, sales office information and management reporting systems need to be explored to establish the output of data. Management should agree:

- what the data should be used for – strategic or tactical decisions
- who should use it – management, staff, etc.
- how it is to be presented – tabular format, graphical format or other ways of analysis relevant to the structure of the business and the market you are in.

The key is to find a way of analysing existing company information with as little paper as possible, but as much fact as can be made available on:

- the current position of the company
- comparison of the past position through trend information showing the development of a period of time
- statistical application of the trend data for forecasting future performance, to predict the way in which the business will grow.

Externally the exploration process relates to establishing what data has to be obtained from other sources, through survey research and data collection:

- Does data exist from published information which adds to managers' understanding of the market, product performance or the effectiveness of marketing?

■ Is there a requirement to customise data to obtain more precise feedback?

This feedback can explore issues of concern that have required a consensus view from management, or can provide new information and a new focus of the issues that have been debated, discussed and are needed to be agreed for managers to take market decisions.

# Searching for data

It is essential to search for existing market information before investing in a specific research study. Why? Because the data you want may have already been collected.

Completing a search will save money, as existing data can be cheaper than the cost of completing a survey. It is also likely to identify the extent of the data that is available, add to the knowledge on which decisions are taken and provide the means to improve managers' understanding of the market, issues or problems that are being evaluated. The search will also add to the design of any specific surveys completed afterwards, as they will be based on existing intelligence. In effect this will help to assess managers' problems, and the issues to be evaluated more precisely.

The time taken to do a search can vary depending on the availability of information:

■ It is generally fast and cost effective in food and drink markets as there is a wealth of published data reports and market monitors.

■ It is usually a detailed and lengthy process in industrial and services sectors, as there are not many available studies and those that have been done need to be reviewed carefully as to their relevance as different sources have to be checked out.

- It is also fast but unproductive in some markets which have little research information, such as the publishing sector, as little data has been collected on an industry-wide basis for publication, and very quickly it is realised that there is nothing of relevance to use.

The searching process therefore lays out the parameters under which a manager can develop the information he/she needs.

7

- A market which already has much data is one which required problem-solving and experimental surveys to be designed and completed by each company in the market.

- A market which has little data is one which requires data on the size, shape and nature of the market, competitor activity in the market and product performance, so that the basic market mechanics can be assessed more precisely.

## Experimenting with survey data

Many managers realise the benefits of research in providing information on what is currently happening in a market. Many managers also fail to use the research techniques available to relate market facts with their own marketing ideas, by testing out their own ideas, product or communications concepts or actual product prototypes. Experimentation is an effective way of reducing the costs of new investments by testing out the options that may relate to implementing the sales and marketing methods that have to provide the return on the investment. However many companies still do not realise the benefits of doing this.

Qualitative research is ideal for the initial input to experimentation as it provides all the techniques of evaluating, interpreting and analysing customers' or users' reactions to products and services. This means experimentation can be exercised effectively as ideas can be tried out, and concepts evaluated, without having to invest in the full market presentation. The research will give an indication of whether the experiment is acceptable or unacceptable, has a positioning or is good in principle, but may need further development to make it user or consumer friendly.

Quantitative research has a range of statistical research methods which test out to what extent experiments are viable in the market. Relating an experiment with a target market, establishing whether the market would buy it and use it, and identifying how much the market would be prepared to pay for it, would be an effective use of quantitative research through experiments. One experiment evaluated in this manner would indicate whether an experiment is right or wrong for a market. Testing out a series of experiments in this way would indicate which ideas are the most viable, which have market potential and which, if developed further, would have a defined and planned market opportunity.

Market experimentation is often less favoured than gaining management commitment to ideas that they have an 'instinct' is right for the market, based on their own knowledge and experience in a market. If research can fulfil an experimentation role then it can make decision making not just more professional, but more certain in the context of the needs and preferences of customers – and could save money being invested in a venture which is not sufficiently consumer oriented.

# Asking questions

The 1980s made consumers more aware of new markets and products because of their ability to afford: it represented a new era of buying based on increased affluence. Consumers have therefore become more sophisticated and have increased their ability for evaluating what is acceptable or unacceptable to them. Linked with this, they have become more able to ask questions and assimilate more information. Research therefore becomes more valuable as there is more knowledge and opinion to assimilate, but this will not be achieved unless the right questions are asked.

9

Research is the focal point of the asking process as its techniques are designed to explore, identify and relate to the issues being asked. Exploring is effective as consumers are asked how they describe a product, a service or a company in relation to competitors. In this situation the exploring process is identifying what 'language' the consumers use to describe the issue being researched. Relating to the issues being asked is to ask consumers whether they agree or disagree with the attitudes and opinions of other consumers, thereby identifying, through the asking process, what is the consensus of opinion.

Managers who are developing sales, marketing and communications decisions are depending on asking consumers what they like or dislike, how they react to ideas and how they relate to other people. Everyone likes to talk about what they do. By asking them with the right questions it can help management to develop 'consumer-led' decisions, but the skill is to design the questions that help management to understand the decision-making process.

# Reflecting on the research findings

The most effective role for market research is to give an objective independent analysis, to provide an indication of what is a true or real situation. This allows management to reflect on what they thought they understood, what is new to them in facts they have learnt, and how they should take on board the implications of the research and the resulting decisions. Research therefore provides management with the key to reflecting on whether they are taking the right or wrong decisions.

In my first book, *The Effective Use of Market Research* (Kogan Page, 1992), I focused on the 'win-win' theory as the conclusion to how research is essential and effective for management. It is an effective tool when you 'win' a first time as the research confirms the prejudices, experiences and pre-conceptions that the management team have about what and how they are doing things. If research achieves this, it also proves and confirms to management that the research has been done correctly.

You 'win' a second time when management learns something new from the research about a market and are able to understand what you are doing, by interpreting a new viewpoint or emphasis which helps to change or improve decisions.

Management 'wins' a third time when both of the two initial

uses of market research are used to impact on the market, refine ideas and strategies and to use research to lead the decision-making process rather than just enhance it. The research then becomes the monitoring tool and is useful for understanding what aspects of the sales, marketing and communications process can be improved to help to increase sales.

This theory has been implemented very effectively by many companies who have started to recognise how research provides guidance for the marketing planning process. Many more companies can benefit too.

Experience shows that this process is the essence of the ability of management to reflect on the market. What is interesting is to see how managers have learnt from this 'win'-'win' theory, reflected on the research data they have collected and have developed more advanced research as a result.

In this book we will therefore focus more on the next important step with using market research – to research and monitor the market – guiding and steering management decisions by collating data which assesses the effectiveness of management performance. This helps to identify who customers are and to find more of the same type of customers. This in essence is the only way to use research as it is the means of growing the business. Once the customers have been found more information and data analysis can be completed to manage the relationship with the customers.

## Collating data

Market research used to be the domain of the specialist, the statistician or numerate management personnel in a company. These technicians were responsible for collecting together published data, and writing short succinct reports which summarised economic, political and market information available in a company. They had the task of classifying the data and filing it into an orderly library of statistics and data reports.

When survey research was commissioned they advised on the technical requirements for the survey, the standard of activity when the project is completed and the validity of the research results when the project was finished. They would then collate the knowledge and information collected in the survey and add it into the Library of Information.

This situation has not changed in most large companies and even in small companies it applies when they have managers who have broad business training. What has changed is the ability for them to collate information. Technological developments and the advanced capability of word processing and databases has been responsible for this change.

In the past only those companies dedicated to market research and the use of data had a marketing information system. Now most computer packages facilitate the means of developing a marketing information system, and this will have an impact on how companies become more oriented to using information and becoming data proficient.

A marketing information system is the means of formalising the coordination process to ensure that data is collected and used. It is the mechanism for collecting data on the trends in the company's markets, the performance of the company within the marketplace, and the opinion of the customers or potential customers at whom it is targeting its products and services. The data is collected and analysed in such a way as to help the company know whether it is taking the right or wrong decisions. A marketing information system ensures that all of the 'vital' information will be collected, analysed and referred to on a continuous basis.

# Hypothesising

Marketing is a common-sense process which depends on making or selling products or services which consumers or users may want or have to buy. It depends on good communications and talking to people in the manner in which you expect others to talk to you about what they buy, what they like and dislike and their behaviour patterns.

13

Effective consumer-led marketing depends on managers being creative, innovative and presenting new ideas to convince consumers that their product is better than that of their competitors. It is not a matter of re-packaging or re-dressing old ideas; it is the requirement to understand how needs change, trends develop and what has become very apparent through the 1980s – consumer sophistication – and how this affects the decisions and aspirations of consumers.

Marketing is all about hypothesising, questioning and thinking about how the products and services must change or be developed to meet the challenge of changing consumer needs. This means asking:

- What if the consumer likes or dislikes the changes?
- What variations of the products are acceptable?
- Which sales, marketing or communications method is the most effective for selling them?

Research has all the statistical techniques to prove or disprove hypotheses and whether the market opportunity exists. The techniques indicate the degree of positive or negative proof towards the hypothesis. But this aspect of hypothesising is less important than the actual recognition that ideas, product concepts, themes for advertising, sales methods, etc., all need to be tested out and researched effectively. The research needs to establish whether your ideas meet the market's needs and whether the market likes or dislikes your ideas.

## Marketing and research working together

To help define what marketing is and to make its purpose clear to managers, the following is quoted from the book *Marketing for Non-marketing Managers* (Pitman Publishing, 1993) written by Patrick Forsyth, with whom I have worked in association regularly over some years and who runs Touchstone Training and Consultancy. It is an excellent book, also in this Institute of Management Series, and can help any manager to understand what marketing is all about.

> Marketing is much more than simply a department – or a body of techniques; it is central to the whole reason for a company's being and its relationship with its market and its customers. While, of course, many activities of a company are important, a commercial organisation can only create profits out in the market, so unless marketing creates a situation where customers buy sufficient product or service at the right price and at the right time, the operation will not be commercially viable.
>
> Marketing has to produce in customers a reason to buy and a more powerful one than any competitor produces; whatever the

many elements involved, the key is to focus on customer needs and set out to satisfy them at a profit.

This definition of marketing shows how important market research is in the marketing process. If marketing is central to the relationship a company has with its market, managers should reject making assumptions about the market and the customers. Research assists in defining what their needs are and helps to evaluate how well managers satisfy their needs. Using research to grow the business in the marketing process is all about understanding why customers buy your products and services and why they prefer them to those of your competitors. What we will see in the rest of this book is the process of making information and research central to running the marketing of a company.

15

## Conclusion

Reviewing data will identify the 'information gaps'. Exploring your data needs will help to define a way of analysing existing company information and identify how and why external data needs to be collected. It is essential to search for existing market information before investing in a specific research project. Completing a search will save money.

Experimentation is an effective way of reducing the costs of new investments by testing out ideas. This makes decision making more effective and more certain once the needs and preferences of customers are understood.

Effective sales, marketing and communications strategies depend on asking consumer questions and taking 'consumer-led' decisions.

Research provides managers with the key to whether they are taking the right or wrong decisions. It needs to become more of a guide to steer management decisions by collecting data which assesses the effectiveness of management performance.

A company needs a marketing information system to ensure that all of the 'vital' information will be collected, analysed and referred to on a continuous basis. 'Using research to Grow Your Business' is the pragmatic way of running a business in the 1990s, as it defines targets and establishes how to look after and grow market segments and the business of the company.

16  What is evident in the 1990s is that both information handling and information management will become extremely important in obtaining competitive advantage, growth and success in business. In 1990 Drucker stated 'information – the right knowledge to take effective action – is still more talked about than used'. However, this might change in the future.

The impact that changes in information management in companies will have on marketing research is only just becoming apparent. In the past, and almost by upbringing, market researchers have been inclined to evaluate roles and positions within the parameters and limits of the research profession. The future of research will change because of the changing role of information within a company.

A new approach to the use of information is going to make it more accessible to all levels of management within a company. This will be acceptable as the situation will respond to a company's need for prescribed or routine analyses or creative, comparative and descriptive analyses which define competitive advantage.

Companies that have realised that using research grows business and has provided benefits have also discovered that information is a strategic weapon which when deployed on a timely basis, does in fact result in sizeable profit gains. With new computer tools becoming available to deliver the information, new opportunities will also arrive for those who take advantage of them. This information will help to drive the business, become more market oriented, more dynamic and more capable of growing their businesses.

# 1

# Key to making good decisions

## Introduction

Fifty years ago, before the market research industry existed, all management took decisions without systematic market analysis or information. Markets and economies were in a different mode and the world was trying to come to terms with its political structure.

After World War Two the economies of the modern era decided to find new markets, new products and new opportunities. Gradually the new-found techniques of political and social research were developed and market and marketing research became a management tool in major corporations.

The 1960s saw a new phase of marketing, using the market segmentation approach, as manufacturers became aware that they had to become closer to the 'markets within markets' and the different characteristics of consumers within a defined market. The 1970s saw the growth of product development and techniques for evaluating the success of communications. The early 1980s was heralded by an increase in the amount of research carried out by service companies. The result of this helped a new trend to emerge in the use of research techniques at the end of the 1980s. Monitoring customer service has become a definitive trend of how companies are using research to determine objectively whether they are doing their jobs well or badly in the eyes of the consumer.

Marketing in the 1990s will be characterised by further innovation through product differentiation and service development. Consumers are becoming older, more pragmatic and more discerning. Marketing will emphasise the 'psychographic' aspects, focusing specifically on their lifestyles and how their needs differ.

In research terms this will see the consolidation of proven techniques, as they will have been established in providing information which management needs. What will be interesting is the fact that more managers in companies will become more dependant on using research techniques as companies become totally 'information oriented' on the 'information highway'. The computer age has exposed more management teams to information than in the past and because of the volume and flow of information in a company, it will become more and more important for management to know how to collect it, collate it, store it, interpret it, analyse it and understand the implications of the facts contained within it.

19

It is therefore essential that management clearly understands what information is and why it is important to take decisions based on facts rather than assumptions. It is also clear that those who do use information for decision making also realise that they take better decisions as a result of using data. The implications of this for management are:

- better knowledge of their markets and the customers they are selling to
- more focused decisions and plans that are realistic to the market
- decisions which assist the company to increase sales by

ensuring that customer needs are met and satisfied.

Information therefore is the key to taking good decisions as it enhances the decision-making process. However, to ensure this is done effectively the meaning of both have to be evaluated.

# What is information?

The real definition of information, as defined by the *Oxford Concise Dictionary* is:

- 'informing'
- 'knowledge'
- 'news'

Research encompasses all of these factors if the breadth of research is appreciated. Information through the adoption of research techniques has a fundamental 'informing' role for management. It relates facts about a product or market which the manager may or may not already know.

Research always improves the 'knowledge' of management as managers need to understand clearly what the needs of the customers are and how these needs are always changing.

Research also provides plenty of 'news' as a well-designed research project will provide facts or facets of situations not clear to management that they are not likely to have known before.

Information, therefore, is something on which management should depend for making good decisions. It is vital in the decision-making process and so key that it is difficult to understand how companies take decisions without information. But many managers will agree that they do.

## Why take decisions with information?

Researchers say that decision making cannot be effectively made without a continuous flow of marketing information and research. Information on your customers and how well you are marketing to them is:

- a reassurance that you know who they are
- providing feedback on how well you are servicing them.

The onus is therefore on management to decide what information is needed to make sure that the decision taken is improved through the use of information.

Management needs to be able to decide:

- What data or information is needed?
- Which decisions will be influenced by this information?
- How is the information to be collected?
- How is the information to be analysed?
- What expenditure is required to collect the information?
- How can a decision be taken without the information?
- Is a wrong decision likely to be taken as a result of not having the information?

The questions above are designed to think through the need for information, define how it will be used, assess the alternatives of having or not having the information, and finally decide the course of action for the decision-making process. This, in essence, is a structural approach to decision making. It is a means of deciding in advance what is required from information collection, rather than taking a decision without the facts. It prevents taking a decision with an interpretation which is more robust than a professional judgement.

Later in the book we will also see that the better the preparation for the research, the better the result that is achieved. Assessment of the information that is needed shapes the nature of the exploratory process that would have to be conducted through market research. Information is therefore giving direction to decision making.

## CASE STUDY

### A contract hire company – making meetings shorter by using good information

The company that learnt how to use information to improve its decisions is in the contract hire sector, providing trucks, cranes, cement mixers and any other equipment required on a building site. The management committee of the company met every month to discuss their activities. The meetings would include members of the Board of the company, sales management, marketing management, production management and research and development management. Ten days prior to the meeting each of the personnel who were attending the meeting were required to submit a report of their activities of the previous month. At the meeting each manager read his report, which only listed what they had done in the last month. The Finance Director would prepare an analysis from the computer tabled at the meeting only, which showed:

- the monthly sales analysis, but as an analysis of the sales of each company in the group

- a comparison with the sales in the same month in the previous year

■ a comparison with the agreed sales targets for the month.

Readers of this book may find this company familiar in that the situation is similar to their own. There is nothing wrong with the approach of this company, as it had functioned this way for a very long time. What was wrong was the management's failure to use the meeting for better planning and to identify how data on the company's performance could help to develop and improve its future performance.

Decisions in this company had been taken from the exchange of 'collected intelligence' collated by managers talking to each other, talking to their staff and talking to their customers. This is essentially not a systematic process.

Changes took place which are easily implemented in any company, provided management allocates the time to set up the systems. Over a period of three months the company accountant produced customised computer material, designed to give management feedback on the discussions they were having at the monthly meeting. The format of this data was much more detailed than before and initially there was concern that there would be more information than could be analysed, digested and understood by the management committee. As these factors were important to a group of managers who were not accustomed to using data, it was agreed only to use this information in the monthly meetings, and to use it in a graphical format which could be easily interpreted.

Each division of the company was provided with a graphical analysis of data which showed:

■ the sales budget for the division over the last two years on a month-by-month basis

■ the actual sales for the division over the same period.

This gave the managers an immediate visual analysis of their per-

23

formance. Not only did it confirm whether sales were on target or not, it would define a 'trend' analysis as to whether the current performance was overall positive or negative to the business.

After three months, as all the managers became used to the system, more information was introduced. The graphical analysis was enhanced by adding information on the various division's types of customer. This new data therefore provided a further management control in that it identified trends within customer types and helped to determine which customer groups needed to be targeted for additional sales activity or customer servicing.

The contract hire company therefore became more 'market oriented' in its decision making and was making better use of internal sales statistics.

## How does information improve decisions?

Information becomes vital to the decision-making process when it is well prepared, used pragmatically, and analysed and interpreted with 'market-led' implications. It improves the decision-making process by reducing uncertainty as well as reducing the amount of assumptions that a team of managers might take. Information therefore allows a more systematic assessment of the facts about a market, or product or any decisions managers take. The keys to making good decisions therefore is to use information, become more analytical in the way it is interpreted, and become dependent on taking the decision when there is fact to support it.

Many companies find it difficult to recognise that information will assist them. Typically these companies may have personnel in them who have worked there for some time and the managers have become used to making 'informed decisions'. Readers of this book may find that they have to persuade their colleagues to use information at all.

## Hints on taking good decisions

*The following are hints on how information helps to make good decisions:*

- *Avoid having meetings in which decisions are taken, without using any company data.*

- *Avoid taking decisions based on past experiences. Markets and customer needs are always changing and information is vital to indicate when these changes are happening.*

- *Extract the data needed to monitor key existing markets and customer groups, but do not generate more data than can be digested and understood quickly from the computer.*

- *Customise the data by making it presentable in a graphic format, which can be easily accessed, interpreted and most importantly updated.*

- *Use the information to plot 'trends' in market and customer groups, and allow all management to be influenced by the data.*

- *Review and revise the format of the data analysis to ensure that the information system is 'dynamic' in relation to the management teams' needs.*

- *Good decisions are information-based. Information is only effective if it is used to indicate whether decisions are right or wrong. The key to making good decisions is to learn how to use information effectively.*

# 2

# Getting the information you really need

## Introduction

Using market research information is a management discipline which needs to be learnt, developed and integrated into a manager's greater understanding of how to manage effectively. Some managers who use it have been heard to say that they spent time and resources collecting the information, but when it had been collected it was just 'a piece of information on which they could not act'. It is these managers who have failed to design, set up and implement the research well. They have failed to be imaginative with their need for information – using it to prove or disprove their ideas. Collecting information in isolation is also likely to be an ineffective way of using research and information, as it is unlikely to relate to the business or management problems.

Market research information injects a flow of data and information into a company. It is constantly collected and it is not always analysed. Extracting this data from the company's databases is as important as collecting it. The key to getting the information a manager really needs – inputting and extracting the essential data – is to develop a marketing information system.

A marketing information system – an MIS – coordinates the collection and extraction process and helps to develop a data-bank of information which is used and acted on. The implication of using a marketing information system is that the company is likely to be more market oriented, using data to guide the decision-making process. In fact a system will:

- control the amount of information a company needs. Efficient system management will ensure that the company collects and uses the data it needs

- need regular evaluation to help management to decide on its needs or data

- be dependant on the computer systems and the use of computer software to make it effective through database marketing, etc.

- need to be supplemented with both *ad hoc* survey research data and continuous and 'one-off' problem-solving data. Survey information such as this is essential for managers to gain a better understanding of the markets in which they operate, as well as the success of their decisions

- become the 'centre of excellence' for the company, the focal point for information, intelligence and statistical background that managers need.

A marketing information system will help a company get the information it really needs as it educates managers

- in what information is essential

- in what data is interesting, but not key to the operating management process.

Marketing information systems therefore make a significant contribution to making research effective in assisting increasing sales.

27

# How to set up systems?

Getting the information you really need depends on the company analysing its customers and markets, as this is crucial for the success of the sales activities. Companies are experiencing that customers are becoming more expensive to reach and therefore it is even more vital to identify the target audiences clearly.

Managers may have experienced the analysis of data by only reading the current reports from their research suppliers. Typically, because of the main emphasis of market research, this process would usually relate to a product launch or an evaluation of a specific marketing problem.

The advantage of a marketing information system is that users can make use of data whenever they need to. In the 1990s, with further technological development, it is likely that data will become more available wherever managers are working.

The marketing information system is divided into two as is shown in the figures 2.1 and 2.2. Figure 2.1 shows the market research content of the system, defining the desk research and the survey research.

Figure 2.2 shows the information needed for monitoring marketing planning, defining what information assists setting marketing objectives, marketing strategies and evaluating marketing tactics.

**Figure 2.1  Marketing information system 1 – market research content**

| Quantitative Information | Desk research | Survey research |
|---|---|---|
| | Market size<br><br>Volumes of sales<br><br>Annual trends<br><br>Seasonal trends<br><br>'State of health' of the market | Demographics of customers and potential customers:<br><br>– owners<br><br>– users<br><br>– buyers<br><br>Products used and preferred<br><br>Price paid<br><br>Purchasing habits<br><br>Lifestyle and background |
| **Qualitative Information** | Market trends<br><br>Performance of products<br><br>Active/inactive segments<br><br>Competitor activity<br><br>Technological development | Consumer needs<br><br>Consumer attitudes<br><br>Consumer preferences<br><br>Attitudes and motivations towards:<br><br>– products<br><br>– prices<br><br>– promotions<br><br>– advertising<br><br>– future purchase<br><br>Comparative competitive evaluation |

29

## Figure 2.2 Marketing information system 2 – Information needed for monitoring marketing planning

| Quantitative information | Marketing objectives | Marketing strategies | Marketing tactics |
|---|---|---|---|
| | Quarterly sales | Product tracking | Sales tracking |
| | Quarterly trends | Market tracking | Advertising tracking |
| | Annual sales | Competitive tracking | Promotion tracking |
| | Quarterly potential | | |
| | Annual potential | | |
| | Current market share | | |
| | Potential market share | | |
| | Quarterly profit | | |
| | Annual profit | | |
| **Qualitative Iinformation** | Reasons for:<br>– trends<br>– sales<br>– potentials<br>– market share<br>– profitability | Market penetration<br><br>New market opportunity<br><br>New product opportunity<br><br>New ideas diversifying the business | Attitude to products<br><br>Assessment of prices<br><br>Evaluation of advertising<br><br>Evaluation of direct marketing<br><br>Evaluation of promotions<br><br>Assessment of sales support<br><br>Assessment of training and back-up and other resources |

The task for managers when deciding how to set up a marketing information system is to decide the following:

- What range of data analysis functions are likely to be needed?

  - segmentation?

  - statistical analysis?

  - forecasting?

  - modelling?

  - regression analysis?

- Can data be imported from other systems – financial, sales, etc?

- What is the volume of data that is needed? Will the system be able to cope with the data?

- What output is needed and how can it be put together for ease of interpretation?

- What frequency of information is needed to provide good data for management reporting?

If these factors are evaluated carefully, a marketing information system will be well designed.

A well-designed system will enhance decisions as they will be better informed. It will help to give a manager a clearer understanding of a company's competitive positioning and its market share. But more importantly, it will improve a manager's ability to identify opportunities and trends in the market. The key element for managers is that they will be able to identify who the customers of the company are, what their buying trends are and what they are likely to want to buy. An automated marketing information system will therefore

31

bring market research closer to a wider range of managers. Output from the system will ensure that a manager is well informed about his market which will ensure that he takes more focused decisions about market development and sales in the future.

The 1990s began with the firm establishment of information technology as a sales and marketing tool for better analysis. A survey by a leading management consultancy in 1993 showed that 70 per cent of companies believe that a marketing database is more important than ever before. Managers are saying that the benefits of these systems are cost savings and increased sales and profitability.

However the survey also gives some important information on the problems managers have experienced in setting up the systems. The rank order of these problems are:

- poorly defined requirements
- a gulf between the marketing and information and technology staff, not understanding each other's needs clearly
- lack of management commitment
- lack of sufficient financial resources
- lack of experience of the potential users of the systems
- problems with systems interfacing within the company.

Marketing information systems are now becoming essential in competitive markets for efficient information management. More and more managers have an improved understanding of how an MIS can be used to support a sales and marketing activity. The result of this is value for money in using information and a better chance of success in monitoring market trends and the needs of customers.

# What internal data is needed in the system?

Information technology has had the effect of involving more and more managers in the use of marketing information and research. Establishing a marketing information system will mean that managers now deal with market data, prospect data and customer data.

Internally, a marketing information system needs to collect, coordinate and disseminate all aspects of internal operating data. This data is the 'marketing intelligence' of a company and it is the control that managers need to run an effective sales and marketing operation. But getting the information you really need in a marketing information system depends on what the information is and how it is used. The following internal operating data are essential:

33

- sales data, presented in a graphic format, can provide regular sales trend information and highlight whether certain customer types need to be targeted or focused

- price information by product line, compared with competitors' pricing but analysed by customer type, to be able to check price trends in customer groups

- stock level data and trends in key accounts or distributors, focusing on whether different outlets need support

- marketing support information, coordinating the effects of marketing promotions, through advertising, direct marketing, trade incentives, consumer competitions, etc.

Every company setting up a marketing information system must customise the data that is entered into the system. Managers must also agree the format of its output, to ensure they understand it, can discuss it and can use it for effective sales and marketing planning.

Some managers would probably see the development of a marketing information system as a company information technology project. If this is so, then there are clear guidelines as to how the project should be completed to be successful. They are:

- **Good communications:** it is important that the sales and marketing staff and the information and technology staff know what is happening in the project and are clear as to the use of the system.

- **Commitment needs to be available from all levels of management:** development of such a system is likely to change the culture of the company, as decisions will be taken in a different manner. It is therefore important that all managers work in unison on the project, and that the lead is taken particularly from senior management. This means at the start of the project that the goals to be achieved are identified and that everyone works together to achieve these.

- **Run the project using an agreed plan:** it is important to agree a 'critical path' for the project, so that no tasks are forgotten.

## What external data is needed?

Whatever marketing intelligence information or internal operating data is needed by a management team, data collected internally is likely to have gaps in it. Opportunities are bound to be identified for additional information, data which is not automatically coming into the company but will enhance the decision-making process.

It is important for a company to 'map' the market in which it exists, to understand the structure of the market and its marketing positioning within it. The questions that need to be answered to develop a customised market map are:

- What is the size of the market in terms of value and volume?

- What is the shape of the market in the context of the distribution structure and intermediaries in the market?

- Are the trends in the market showing an increasing, static or declining market?

- What is the nature of the competition and how does our company differ from them?

- Which customers buy and what do they prefer and which other buying groups are potential customers?

- Which sales, marketing and communications methods are used and which of these are successful?

- How satisfied are our customers with our products and services and how does this compare with competitors?

However, a management team that is interested in using market research to increase business needs to evaluate what aspects of external data should be collected to supplement the internal information. This relates specifically to:

- setting the company's marketing objectives

- defining the essential marketing strategies

- establishing the effective marketing tactics to implement the strategic marketing plan.

35

# Quantitative information – evaluating marketing objectives

The essential marketing information to set the marketing objectives and to be able to appraise and review them on a regular basis are:

- sales statistics analysed on a quarterly and annual basis
- market share information by geographical and business market
- financial performance both quarterly and annually.

## Assessing marketing strategies

As we will see later in the book, marketing strategies can be set if the company has regular survey information tracking products, defining trends in markets and evaluating product performance in a competitive tracking analysis.

## Tracking marketing tactics

This survey can also monitor the effectiveness of the marketing tactics by tracking advertising awareness and recall, other promotions tracking and buyers' attitudes to all sales methods used.

## Qualitative information

Many companies are satisfied with using quantitative information as it gives them independent facts and data on the market. It gives enough information to plan marketing and monitor its effectiveness. However, it lacks vital information giving the reasons for the facts that have been found, and more importantly, the attitudes of the current and potential market towards the products or services the company provides. Qualitative information provides this key additional input to decision making.

## Evaluating marketing objectives

Marketing objectives can be set effectively if the reasons behind the trends in the market are understood. Understanding why there is a market potential and what are the competitive reasons for a market share help a company to define the marketing objectives and the task to increase sales to improve company profitability.

Setting marketing strategies needs a clear understanding of the options offered by each strategy and the likely results of choosing one option in preference to another. Researching the competitive positioning in the market by determining penetration in the market will help to define a market penetration strategy, to enter more of the market and increasing market share.

## Assessing marketing objectives

If a marketing objective has been to find new markets to enter, research can assist by evaluating the reasons why new customers might buy the company's products or services. Equally, if markets are to segment effectively into different types of customer, each with different needs, then a new market opportunity might be identified as a potential opportunity in one of the segments.

Researching the reasons why a product is or is not liked by consumers can help to define new product improvements and thus a new product opportunity. Marketing strategies for new product opportunities can also be evaluated if new product ideas, product concepts, product prototypes and test products are given to current and potential customers to test out. Usually an existing product is paired with a product concept and consumers are asked to test out each one and say which they prefer. This is more commonly known as a paired comparison test. Sometimes one concept is tested against another concept to see which is preferred. This helps a company to prioritise product opportunities or, in some instances, eliminate options that are unattractive to customers.

Research is vital in strategic evaluation if new ideas for diversifying the business are evaluated or tested out. A company entering a new market with a new product is unlikely to know much about that market and is going to be dependent on good information for decision making for developing sales of the new product and services. The research is likely to reduce the uncertainty about pursuing the diversification opportunity and to help managers to plan, based on known and defined customer needs.

## Evaluating marketing tactics

Research techniques in the 1980s were developed by managers to evaluate marketing tactics and now, in the 1990s, this aspect of market research is being used effectively. Qualitative evaluation of tactics has a direct effect on how these tactics are developed and used to increase sales.

Good evaluation qualitatively, to establish customers' attitudes and motivations towards the way a company organises its marketing tactics, can be used in the quantitative surveys designed to track marketing tactics. Usually this is done through the development of attitude statements in the qualitative research and then applying the statements to the target customers by getting them to agree or disagree with them when assessing the marketing methods.

There are three different types of marketing tactic that can be assessed effectively through market research.

## ATTITUDE TO PRODUCTS

Research into attitudes and motivations towards products help managers to understand the consumer 'terminology' towards the products. In effect, it is the way in which consumers describe a product, i.e. the language they use, that can be used to promote the product to other consumers. Consumer descriptions of a product such as 'Easy to bite', 'Appetising' and 'Healthy' are ways in which a product can be assessed and indicates consumers' likes and dislikes for it.

## ASSESSMENT OF PRICES

Qualitative research helps managers to understand price acceptability and the way in which a consumer evaluates and measures prices. Actual price paid compared with value for money needs to be assessed to understand consumers' attitudes to the purchase. Once this has been done consumers are also receptive to discussing how price changes can affect their purchase decisions.

**EVALUATION OF ADVERTISING AND PROMOTIONS**

Communications concept evaluation and acceptance is the most applied use of qualitative techniques. Many advertising agencies use the technique to prove or disprove the creative ideas that they have developed for advertising campaigns. The limitations of this approach are to confirm ideas that may not relate totally to customers' needs and particular types of customer in a market. It is likely also to focus on short-term requirements for a product and to concentrate on the fundamental needs and purchase decisions taken by a consumer when buying a product.

40

A more effective use of qualitative techniques for communi-cations development and evaluation is to use the research to:

- identify which features of the product or service the con-sumers are aware of and associate with

- determine what benefits of the product or service are realised and appreciated by the consumers

- test out themes and concepts which communicate the benefits to the potential customers, the features of which are highlighted in the advertising. Benefits are best com-municated with slogans or strap lines, which in an amus-ing or direct manner, tell the customer why he or she will benefit from buying the product. These also should be tested out for their suitability and fit with customers.

## CASE STUDY

### A private bank – using information to target customers

Private banks have traditionally found their customers by having them referred to them by other very satisfied customers. This means that their main contact with customers is not through the disciplines and techniques of sales and marketing but primarily through high quality customer service. But the 1990s has started with a situation where the financial markets and the financial services sector have become very competitive with many companies offering similar facilities and services. It is therefore difficult for financial services organisations to find more of their traditional type of customer, let alone expand a new customer base of people who may have become more attracted to, or more eligible for, their services.

The Private Bank recognised that it could not develop a sales and marketing plan without good information to give it direction on how to promote and market its services. But what did it know about its customers, and how could this understanding of the customer base help to find new customers?

The unfortunate facts were that it did not have any data with which it could carry out a systematic analysis of the customer base and the potential market. So to get the information it really needed it had to develop a system for setting up the customer analysis.

The Bank had developed a customer records system which collected much of the personal details about a customer which aided the organisation to provide the high quality customer service. However, few of the managers took care in filling in the details and updating the records, and those who did only carried out the task as a formality to record the last customer contact, rather than to make a contribution to the development of the sales and marketing system.

The extent of the data collected about a customer is seen in Figure 2.3 which is an extract of the computer output from a customer record card. It can be seen from this that there is more than enough information to develop an overall analysis. This analysis would define who is the present customer base and highlight certain characteristics which could be used in deciding to whom to promote the service.

## Figure 2.3 Bank internal information system

| | |
|---|---|
| Name: | Type: |
| First: | Status: |
| Family Name: | Security: |
| | Priority: |
| | Net worth: |
| | Income: |

| | |
|---|---|
| Business Name: | A/c Executive |
| Occupation: | Officer: |
| Family Name: | Introduced by: |
| Occupation: | Manner of |
| | introduction: |
| Nationality: | Prospect for further |
| | introduction: |
| Birth Date: | |

| | |
|---|---|
| Last Contact: | Result: |
| Next Call: | Result: |
| Next Visit: | |
| Achieved: | |
| Planned: | |

| | |
|---|---|
| Home Address: | Phone: |
| | Fax: |
| Postcode: | Telex: |
| Location: | E-Mail No: |
| Acorn Area: | |

| | |
|---|---|
| Business Address: | Phone |
| | Fax: |
| Postcode: | Telex: |
| Location: | E-Mail No: |

The Bank had not taken advantage of the data on the computer and expressed concern that it did not know who to contact to sell the Bank's facilities and financial services. Analysis of the data would:

- define the characteristics of the present customer by

  - age

  - income

  - occupation

- establish the concentration of the customer base geographically

- identify who referred them to the Bank to establish whether there was any particular type of person who tended to refer people to such a Private Bank.

43

The result of this analysis gave the Bank sufficient information to decide who to target:

- high income earners in professions – accountants, solicitors, barristers, management consultants, landowners and property developers

- people who live in certain post code areas of London, Surrey, Sussex, Buckinghamshire and Hertfordshire (defined later in the book as the Geodemographic areas 34 and 36 of the Acorn analysis)

- the 35–54 age group who are in the mid and late family lifestages.

This profile therefore enabled the sales staff, for the first time, to isolate the particular type of person who was likely to become a potential customer of the Bank.

The Bank also decided to carry out a survey among customers to establish what benefits they felt were achieved by being a customer of the Bank. In-depth interviews were completed with both private and commercial customers. What was interesting was the degree to which the style of customer service influenced the customers' attitudes towards the Bank. It was not just that it was perceived to be better than other Banks, it was the fact that the Bank delivered good customer service consistently that was important to the customer. The findings of the survey were input into the marketing information system and used to monitor the consistency and quality of customer service standards.

The result of this initiative was to use geodemographic data in the areas of the country identified and to develop a telephone marketing campaign backed by personal visits. Brochures were also developed which featured the importance of consistent customer service. The campaign was launched at a time when Bank services were being scrutinised so the timing had good results in attracting customers who met the criteria of the Banks' customer profile.

# Developing trend information

Many companies are now more used to referring to customer profile information because of database packages marketed with computer systems software. Getting the information you really need from these databases depends on manipulating the output of the data from the computer to get it to tell a story.

Referring to the data on a monthly basis and comparing the analysis of that month with the same period in the previous year, two years, three years or more is just a 'snap shot'. This picture only informs a manager that he/she is doing better or worse than before and it does not give sufficient indication as to the action he/she should take.

If this data is analysed in either tabular or graphic format over a longer time period, say one or two years, then trends start to be identified and it makes the information meaning-ful. At a glance a manager can see the pattern of the statistics – increasing, remaining static or declining – and without any further difficulty can start to make decisions about the appropriate actions. This method is also effective from the point of view of keeping the volume of data down and ensuring that those who are not used to being analytical can start to use data for good decision making.

Later in the book we will be discussing the most effective techniques in survey research for assisting managers to use data to increase sales. The principle of trend information in these surveys applies in the same way as for internal information. However, there are important techniques to review for these surveys. The most important aspect to appreciate is to recognise that effective and actionable survey information can only be collected if surveys are carried out over a series of time periods, plotting trends and monitoring needs of customers.

45

## Targeting through database marketing

The increasing use of computers has caused the development of *database marketing*, which includes the growth of *lifestyle databases* and *geodemographics*. Linked with this, the growing activities of database marketing has encouraged institutions to develop customer databases. In financial institutions this has required a change of focus from account-based computer systems to customer-based databases.

All of this is bound to grow in the future as institutions become totally computer dependant and managers develop further their analytical skills to decision making. In association with this:

- geodemographics will provide further customer data to be linked with internal information as the classification systems become meaningful in reality to account usage, policy purchase or investment decision making

- developments in both hardware or software will provide the 'window' of opportunity for management to improve their skills

- geographic information systems, digital mapping-based databases will provide institutions with even more focused abilities to target customers in a more localised way and plot demand geographically.

This also means that management will become more sophisticated in their needs for information and internal and external data will integrate into the marketing information system and the companies' management information system. The result will be the reality that the MIS is the focal point of strategy development and monitoring sales, marketing and communications methods.

### Hints about getting the information you really need

- *It is important for managers to realise that the company needs to develop an 'information culture' and become analytical in its approach to decision making.*

- *Defining what data is needed internally and externally establishes essential data.*

- *Develop a marketing information system, but customise it to the company, its product range and the markets in which it operates.*

- *Present internal data in a format that is easy to interpret, preferably graphic.*

- *Decide what survey data is needed and plan it in a series of research phases designed to provide trend information related to the buying habits and needs of customers.*

- *Hold a series of management workshops to discuss how the information should be used.*

- *Generate data which helps to plan and monitor marketing objectives, marketing strategies and marketing tactics.*

47

# 3

# The best research techniques anyone can use

## Introduction

**M**arket research has two important functions for managers. They are:

- to reduce any uncertainty that managers might have in taking decisions, by giving them intelligence, statistics and information on which to base the rationale for the decisions they take

- to monitor the sales and marketing decisions that have been taken, to identify whether they were right, whether they need to be revised and whether they need total rethinking.

Using market research to increase sales depends on developing a systematic market research programme, customised for a company and integrated into the management planning system. The key to using this research programme effectively is to do the following:

- develop a sales, marketing and communications strategy with detailed actions for its implementation

- develop a series of ideas that can be evaluated through research and proved or disproved as to whether they would help to develop the strategy

- develop a database on the size, shape and nature of a market and its structure, to understand the environment in which the managers are taking their decisions

- assess the acceptability of the company's products in the market and the understanding of the advertising and promotions in the potential customer base to target sales, marketing and communications effectively.

If this is completed by any company then the management team will have sufficient data to decide on the actions it can take after the research. Further research would assess the success of these actions and identify what other actions are important to take. Managers therefore can use research findings to improve the ways in which sales, marketing and communications methods are organised by the company. This whole process helps to develop a company's products and communications in such a way that they correspond to the buying behaviour of customers and potential customers.

49

But the difficulty with market research is that it is complex and involves using techniques which, if used incorrectly, may not provide information which is actionable. Some people who have used research techniques which were not planned well will have found that the research they have done ends up as a piece of information. This information might be correct as a series of facts, but often managers find that the research is not of use to them as they cannot decide what actions to take as a result of reading the data – it may also not help to identify a trend.

The best techniques that any manager can use depend on the research being developed, planned and implemented effectively. In planning, the more time that is taken in discussing how the research will be carried out, the better the research will be. This applies particularly to the development of a questionnaire, as reviewing its structure, agreeing the phraseology of the questions and thinking about how the results of the research will be used, will have a direct influence on the quality of the questionnaire that is used. In its implementation, the longer the time the project takes the better the quality of the result, as the interviewing will have been done carefully, the analysis of the data completed with precision and the interpretation of the results reasoned in the context of market trends or customer needs. A good research project is likely to be implemented well since the results of the research will be clear to managers and the answers to the questions will provide immediate direction, allowing decisions to be taken. A manager cannot go wrong if he/she proceeds in a definite pattern to carrying out research.

Before any survey research is carried out, it is important to establish whether any published data would solve the sales, marketing or communications problem or help to take the right decisions. Any survey that is designed by a manager is not likely to be planned well unless the manager can under-stand the emphasis or positioning of the company or its prod-ucts in the market. Brand share data would help in this respect but it needs to be linked with a trend analysis to understand the performance of the company or its products in the market.

Once these issues have been evaluated and developed then a manager will have the rationale for designing a specific sur-vey. Having referred to published and brand share data, the manager is more likely to design a better survey as the research will have taken account of the key issues in the market.

# Collecting published data

Any manager, budget conscious and cauticus of developing an information system which does not contain the right information, will want to collect existing published information before commissioning special projects. Data may already exist which answers a marketing, communications or sales problem or provides a further insight into a situation which helps to design the analysis needed to solve the problem. The best technique to use when exploring published information is to follow a procedure which gives reassurance that all possible sources of information are explored, evaluated and, if necessary, eliminated.

51

First, check the information that exists in your own company. Past managers may have carried out some research and the findings of it, although possibly out of date, may provide an indication of the issues related to the problem or market analysis being considered. Also try to develop a 'centre of excellence' for all this published data, as a library or information unit. If there is published data already in the company, it must be accessible by all levels of management. I was once completing a survey for a company and at one of the review meetings a senior manager said he had found a report which gave an account of a similar project but it was ten years out of date. When I explained to the manager that it would be useful as it provided 'benchmark' data against which the new data could be compared, he apologised for not bringing it from his home earlier in the discussions. This manager did not realise the importance of keeping that data in the office in a central information system.

Many companies are recognising the investment in information that they are making, and are using the resources of new

technology to provide an effective internal database on published information. An example of this is a multi-national
financial services company which runs a central information
facility on its computer which is accessible by any manager
in any of its offices worldwide. Any internal or externally
commissioned project is recorded in this system by writing a
short summary in the computer entry showing:

- the country in which the research is carried out
- the target market researched
- the objectives of the research project
- the research method used

- the key findings of the research and important data that is
  regularly monitored in all research projects to update
  trend analyses
- the implications of the research and which managers
  would need to take actions as a result
- the actions taken, and any issues learnt as a result, which
  would be helpful in ensuring that the project is improved if
  commissioned again at a later date.

The reasons why this organisation finds that the users are
pleased with the system say that using the data 'does very
nicely' is because data can be accessed quickly, the data gives
an insight into an issue or problem at the time it is being discussed at a touch of a button, and because it helps to ensure
that future research is planned better and more effectively.

If internal data does not assist then the next phase is to refer
to external information. Business libraries, on-line search
systems, universities, research institutes and trade associations are all key sources of information for any of the following:

- government statistical publications
- annual company reports and accounts
- official statistics, UK government data, EC, OECD and UN statistics
- directories, annual year books, industry lists and classifications
- market reports
- stockbrokers reports
- market reviews such as:
  - Frost and Sullivan
  - EIU
  - Mintel
  - Dun and Bradstreet
  - Forbes
  - Donnelly
  - Find/SVP.

There is also an excellent directory called *Market Search* (Arlington Publications), which is a complete listing of all product categories. Under each category heading is listed all the published reports on that category worldwide, identifying its cost and who published it. Each entry provides the title of the report, a brief synopsis of what the report is about, the number of pages, and the cost of the report. The entries are coded by the publishing company and cross referencing the code with the list of companies at the back of the book yields the name, address, telephone and fax numbers of each of the companies. More details about the reports, order forms, etc., can be obtained from the companies.

Although the data a manager may be lacking is not identified through an exhaustive evaluation of published data, contact with all possible data sources allows your name to be put on mailing lists and updates can be sent to you to help identify any new data in the future that would be of use.

# Using brand share data

Many industries only use sales statistics on which to measure sector performance, product performance and competitor activity. Government data and manufacturers' sales data is often collected, analysed and disseminated by trade and industry associations on behalf of the industry and members of these associations. This is an effective way of understanding:

- the size of the market
- trends in the market
- who the market leaders are
- which product sectors are performing well
- domestic versus overseas business segments.

In some sectors, such as the insurance sector, the pharmaceutical sector, the carpet sector, the automotive sector manufacturers supply their sales data to an independent objective analysis company. The data is entered into a computer and an analysis developed. Each participant to the brand share data exchange gets the following data:

- information on the size of the market
- their sales in relation to the total sales in the market
- their brand shares by each product category.

This data is very useful for developing competitive product strategies, setting objectives of increasing market share and identifying where certain product sectors need regenerating and developing.

We will see later in the book how monitoring market shares becomes important for tracking trends in markets. Some sectors have developed procedures for brand share monitoring. These include:

- a retail audit or consumer panel which are used to monitor brand shares:
  - A retail audit is based on selecting a representative sample of retail outlets which represent the volume of business transacted through all of the outlets. A retail audit is very useful as, apart from providing the method for recording the sales and brand shares, it can be used as a mechanism for assessing the product penetration and distribution achieved.
  - A consumer panel will be set up by recruiting a group of private households and interviewing a member of the household. The consumer panel can be used to develop data and information which describes the types of consumer responding to the products, product purchase and whether they are likely to buy the product again.
- developing predictive models which are usually set up by analysing three types of data:
  - penetration data: the proportion of buyers in the population who purchase a product
  - repeat purchase data: the proportion of buyers in the population who purchase a product again
  - a buying rate factor: a weighting factor that is added to

55

the analysis to assess whether the buying process is an average purchase or not.

# Developing customer data

Good managers are those who are analytical, ready to question their decisions and receptive to testing out ideas and using information to influence their decisions. However, the type of data we have reviewed so far is not likely to help good managers to achieve this ideal situation, as the data collected is unlikely to be sufficiently specific or relevant to the decisions that need to be taken. It is therefore essential and interesting to managers to be able to create, design and initiate their own tailor-made surveys to help them approach their sales, marketing and communications decisions with information-based confidence.

However, the process of developing customer data is a complex procedure of initiating a company 'culture' towards using information and also deciding on, developing, modifying and running systems that relate to the whole satisfying process of the company's present and potential customers. The cultural development also relates to management procedures in the short and long term and how the data becomes integrated into the company and its management procedures.

In the short term, it is a matter of seeing what data is already available as reviewed earlier in this chapter. It is also important to review a number of factors to agree what customer data is needed. Management has to establish what assumptions it has taken, and decide how it has to understand the market and customer needs more clearly. It also has objectively to come to terms with recognising that it has to decide what new information it ought to use to learn about its customers. The third and the most challenging action it has to take is to think about what customers might or might not like, new product or communications ideas, and 'hypotheses' about how customers might react to new approaches or ideas made by the company. And, as many companies do not use research in this way, it is important for changing the whole philosophy of the company.

In the longer term, the management team has to decide what regular information is needed about customers, to identify any trends that might emerge in the market. It also has to understand customers' attitudes and how they change, their behaviour and how it can be influenced, and how certain segments of the market become regular or loyal customers for specific reasons. The most effective customer databases also can provide an early warning system to establish if customers' attitudes or behaviour is changing and if competitor activity causes changes or differences in market activity.

57

The key to developing customer data that becomes effective information for increasing sales is to classify the customer base, using definitions which characterise the customer in the marketplace. Consumer markets are generally classified by defining the consumers according to their age, sex and social class (or income), depending on which consumer classification system is used.

Industrial markets are classified by the type of organisation in the context of its international industrial classification, the size of the company in terms of its turnover, number of employees and whether it is a new company, developing company or well established in its particular segment.

The interesting fact about these classification systems is that they are unlikely to help to increase sales. They are more likely to tell you about your customers, who they are, where they are, what they want, what they like or dislike. For industrial customers it will tell you who they are, where they are and what they like or dislike, but it will also establish how they buy, why they buy and who should be influenced in the buying process.

Managers who become more experienced in developing customer data have been able to improve on the standard classification systems and develop customer characterisations which are more relevant and more appropriate for their businesses. This includes classifying data by their various contacts with and knowledge of your company and its product and services.

Customers divide into:

- current customers, who need to be defined as to how satisfied they are with your products and services

- potential customers, who need to be persuaded to use your products and services

- owners and users, who need to be monitored for their usage of the products to establish whether the product benefits were delivered

- buyers, who may not be the users but who have a clear attitude towards the competitive positioning of the products and services, having taken a decision to buy your product in preference to competitors' products.

In the 1980s a whole new industry grew up through the geo-demographics industry. This has developed census-based geodemographics, lifestyle- or credit-based data into becoming marketing information resources. The benefit of using these systems is to customise them on your company's computer system. This will be discussed in more detail in the next chapter.

## CASE STUDY

### A map, atlas and travel guide publisher – using research techniques to monitor the market

The publishing sector has only become oriented to using research in the last ten years. Traditionally used to using sales data as the measure of customer monitoring, it lacked the opportunity for effective branding and targeting to its customers. But to the map, atlas and travel guide publisher the customer was the bookshop – the distributor – rather than the buyer, user or reader of the product. There had been no market analysis to define the characteristics of the current and potential customer, and therefore no help for bookshops to promote and sell to the right customer to achieve sales. There also had been no information to establish trends in the market to help publishers allocate and set product development and promotional budgets to capitalise on the changing customer needs.

59

A group of map, atlas and travel guide publishers decided to collaborate to develop a research group to provide cost effective research. In this way an individual publisher could share industry data, but apply an analysis to it which would relate to its own specific needs. Two specific studies were set up annually which have become central to a publisher's sales, marketing and communications planning.

An annual trade survey was developed to monitor sales, marketing and communications with the publishers traditional customer, the bookshop. Rather than just confirm what a publisher already knew

about this type of customer, the database asked bookshops to provide feedback on the sales, marketing and communications support
provided by a publisher.

The benefit of this to the publishers using this data has been to evaluate the nature of their support while comparing it with that of their
competitors. In addition, over a period of years, they are able to monitor whether the support they are providing is consistent and, if
changes need to be made, where budget allocations can be provided.

A quarterly household survey was also set up to define the users and
buyers, non-users and non-buyers of each of the product categories.
This survey assessed which products they bought, where they
bought them, awareness of publishers and their marketing, their
travel patterns, and use and purchase of the products when travelling.

The benefit of this survey to the publishers has been to provide a
profile of the present and potential customer base, confirming the
targets to concentrate on to increase their sales. In addition, the trend
analysis has allowed the publishers to view product development
and market development in a more systematic and structured manner. Prior to using the data, most of the publishers viewed the products as one overall category – maps, atlases and guides only –
distinguishing between them when a new series or title launch was
developed. The consumer survey trends showed that the profile and
buying habits of consumers for each product category was different,
implying that marketing methods needed to be applied to each as a
segment in their own right. The map segment had a broad socio-economic profile, but purchase was concentrated in the 25–34 age
group. The atlas segment is also broad in socio-economic profile, but
purchase and use is spread from under 18 to 55+. The travel guide
segment is a defined market, mainly up market and in the 35–44 age

group. The result of this analysis was a complete change in management decision making towards each segment of the market, for cost-effective targeting.

---

# Customising research techniques

The approach shown in the case study above is not unusual to a number of industry sectors, especially the food, drink, travel and financial services sectors. The surveys described are essentially industry surveys, providing the background to the market, the performance in the industry and the key trends that exist. Companies in these industries have learnt to use the profile of the consumers in the database, the incidence of buyers and non-buyers and the awareness of the companies and their brand in the sector to develop customised databases.

Generally there are two types of survey that provide specific data for these companies. They are as follows:

- user and attitude surveys, usually known as 'U & A'. These tend to be surveys among product users, relating the profile of these consumers with 'attitude' statements which are used to describe what they like or dislike about the products

- awareness and attitude surveys, surveys which monitor competitive awareness of brands and manufacturers, also linking them with 'attitude statements' used to describe what they like or dislike about the products.

However, it is only after these surveys have been run at least twice that these databases become effective. When used in conjunction with the general industry surveys, marketing

61

information can be used to relate to specific management and marketing issues. We will see in the next chapter how customising measurement techniques achieves this.

## Getting the marketing language correct

As research has a primary objective of reducing risk by understanding what a market wants and how potential customers are likely to react to a product or service offered, it is important to relate all of the findings to the sales, marketing and communication strategy. A good manager will want these strategies to relate to the target customer and be oriented to the different customer types that exist in the target group. There are two research techniques that provide the right data and feedback to orientate marketing effectively.

The first is to add into a questionnaire 'open-ended' questions which allow the respondent – a customer or a potential customer – to express their opinions on what they like or dislike or what is their attitude to the subject being evaluated. The answer given to the question by the respondent will give an indication of the attitudes, motivations, reasons and 'true reaction' to the market, product or service. The best technique to use in research to identify how to increase sales through a customer-oriented strategy is to use this questioning process in two stages.

Initially, qualitative research is carried out to make the most of the evaluation process to establish 'Why', 'What', 'How', 'When' and 'Which', on all comments that are made by the informant. This allows for a very detailed exploration of current buying habits, reasons for purchase and usage, and non-purchase and non-usage, and gives the manager the means of identifying how this background relates to the strategy being proposed. The results of this initial stage are therefore analysed with regard to how it helps a manager to focus the strategy more specifically. But in doing so there will be an urgent need to establish how significant these findings are to determine the priorities for implementing the strategy.

The second stage is to quantify the findings by asking many more informants about the issues researched and identified in the first stage. A quantitative study is seen by some as just to confirm the findings of the qualitative phase by gaining agreement positively or negatively to the questions asked. However, this answer is not likely to be a detailed analysis or interpretation, and by limiting the answer to just 'Yes' or 'No' the manager could miss some of the context of the interpretation of the results.

The second technique is to create 'attitude' or 'image' statements which are used to establish the extent to which agreement is made to the questions asked. 'Attitude statements' are phrases or sentences which relate to the attitudes, motivations, purchase and usage criteria which are identified in the qualitative research. They are specifically phrased in the consumer 'language' to help the strategy planner to orient the decisions in consumer terms. 'Maps are a hassle to us', or 'I do not want to travel with a map as I do not want to look like a dumb tourist' are attitude statements that have been created from an analysis of qualitative research. Image statements are similar but they relate to the image of the company, awareness of the company's activities via its marketing, or reaction to advertising, point-of-sale promotions, catalogues, direct mail or any other sales and marketing materials used by the company – 'forward looking product development', 'creative advertising'.

The research technique is to ask informants to say whether they agree or disagree with the statement, or use an important to an unimportant rating, to get the appropriate reaction to the statement being asked. Using a five-point bi-polar scale – two positive ratings, Agree and Agree Strongly, two negative ratings, Disagree and Disagree Strongly, and a don't know rating, Neither Agree nor Disagree – the research analysis provides useful data. Two analyses can be achieved from this technique. A percentage response analysis based on the total number of interviews and how many respondents agree or disagree with the statement. The other analysis is a mean (average) analysis based on the bi-polar (+2 to –2) rating which gives an average response to the rating. When you have a 'battery' of statements – a group of statements in one question – the average analysis can provide a ranking of statements which can be useful if there is a series of statements assessing attitudes or motivations.

An effective way of using this technique to ensure that the analysis is in the right language is to pose the question as though the consumer was in a conversation. The introduction to the question can imply that, as others have made a comment, it is useful to get a reaction – 'Some people have made comments as to why they have bought maps. Looking at the statements listed on the questionnaire, please tell me whether you agree or disagree with them'. This relates to the informant and makes them feel that they are involved in the subject.

Attitude and image statements are the key to making research relate to marketing and communications planning. If research is carried out regularly, then they can be used to monitor attitude and image change and become an essential part of the research monitoring process. In recent years they have also been used for customer monitoring programmes and their use in these has allowed more managers to benefit from this technique and how customer monitoring can influence strategy development and decision making.

Elsewhere in the book we have referred to the application of techniques and their influence on management and how they are used for planning. Attitude statements are an essential part of the application of techniques. Once quantified in a two-stage study, they have laid the 'benchmark' when used again to compare how attitudes change or establish trends.

Factor analysis can also be applied to the evaluation of the data collected from attitude statement assessment. Computer generation of the statistical analysis using the appropriate statistical package correlates the attitudes of the informants and identifies a structure to the opinions given. This type of analysis assists the manager to advance from using standard socio-economic analysis to learning about and classifying the market in the context of both positive and negative attitudes and motivations.

Cluster analysis is a further approach to multivariate analysis, examining the relationships among a number of variables. This statistical technique aims to identify groups of individuals who have relatively similar characteristics and distinguishes these from any other individuals identified. So having established the number of factors or attitudes and motivations through the factor analysis, the cluster analysis helps to define a specific target market or develops an effective market segmentation.

The key benefit of segmentation is to divide a market into parts, each of which has identifiable characteristics whether they are of the product or service or the user or buyer of the product.

### Hints on using the best research techniques

- *Decide on how to reduce uncertainty in decision making by recognising that published research and external surveys can provide both interesting and actionable information.*

- *Take as much time as possible and as long as is practicable for the discussion and development of the research. The longer that planning is carried out, the better the result of the project.*

- *Published information should be collected to add to the 'intelligence' in the company, but do not depend on it as the key to decision making. It is likely not to be totally relevant or sufficiently accurate to relate it to the sales, marketing or communications plan.*

- *Link the data generated on your computer with published data, as this will provide sufficient information to develop trend data, based on company performance analysis (actual sales, etc.). Add to it the key findings of your regular survey research and it will provide the benchmark for an interactive marketing intelligence system.*

- *Use brand share data to indicate the effectiveness of sales and marketing methods. The brand share analysis should be viewed as the early warning system for further market analysis depending on the brand movements identified.*

- *When profiling the market through survey research ensure there are sufficient questions in the questionnaire to sub-segment the target groups into useful analyses. Do not do what a retailer did recently in trying to segment their market. They chose to divide it into heavy, medium and light buyers based on the number of products they bought (heavy – ten plus products, medium – five to ten products, light – one to four products). This is less effective than making these definitions based on use and purchase, as it does not give any information on buying habits and the frequency of buying. A better classification of purchase may be as follows:*

– *Heavy:*    *a few times a year or more frequent*

– *Medium:*  *once a year to one and a half years*

– *Light:*     *once every two years or less frequent.*

*Usage may be classified as follows:*

– *Heavy:*    *once a week or more*

– *Medium:*  *a few times a month*

– *Light:*     *few times every six months/a few times a year or less.*

■ *Customising data means analysing the research in relation to the sales decisions, marketing plans and communications strategies that are being developed.*

# 4

# What to measure and how to measure it

## Introduction

**T**he task of data collection is not complete until a manager has turned the information that is collected in the research into actionable facts, that lead on to conclusions and then practical recommendations that help to take decisions that enable the company to increase sales. There is a sequence to this data analysis process.

First, the data has to be 'edited' and 'coded'. Editing removes omissions, errors and also provides the opportunity to find inconsistencies. Coding is the method for deciding on how the data is assembled into common factors, which can be analysed and entered into the computer, and used to inter- pret sales and marketing actions.

Managers should not really decide what to measure until the basic analysis techniques are applied, to see whether the classification information provides a meaningful analysis. This provides the data user with the first results of the research, and establishes whether the market can be seg- mented, or certain sub-groups show any strength of opinion in the market. Typically, this can be achieved by providing one computer tabular analysis for each question being analysed from a questionnaire. (See Appendix II – Computer Analysis.)

It is only once these tabulations have been reviewed a manager can decide on applying statistical techniques which help to understand the facts that have been collected in a more meaningful way. If a survey is carried out regularly, then the applied techniques can be run at the initial analysis of the new survey and updated for each of the following surveys.

The most efficient manager will want to evaluate some options for what to measure and how to measure the data. These include the following:

- **Identifying segments from the results.** Data analysis can identify the size and nature of sub-groups of the population. It can confirm how the sub-groups buy and use products and their attitudes to the companies manufacturing and selling them. As markets become more 'global', the segmentation analyses will be used more frequently as they are important in establishing what similarities and differences exist in markets in the global village. The advantage of global marketing is to be able to find similarities in the different markets the company is operating in.

- **Using data for forecasting.** Existing data can be analysed with past data, trends can be identified and highlighted and then a forecast developed by projecting the trend forward. When forecasts have been proven to be useful, then more detailed forecasts can be developed by developing 'market models', which make assumptions that there are relationships with the data being forecast and factors that have influence on the data – economic, political or financial factors, for example.

- **Applying forecasting models to the data.** Data which does not show any trend or seasonality is most effectively analysed by applying forecasting models such as moving

69

averages. Seasonal patterns are best evaluated through special techniques for 'exponential smoothing'.

- **Using attitude and behaviour models.** These include 'trade-off' models, pricing models and test market models. Conjoint analysis is effective for analysing experimental data. It models the decision process that consumers take when selecting a product or service, and relates their own data to the decision process.

  Price modelling provides all the facts about buyers and relates consumers' reactions to pricing, establishing the most acceptable price to the buyers. Test market models forecast the potential for a new product, by estimating brand share depending on variations of the marketing mix.

- **Using data fusion.** This is 'fusing' together data from two surveys or even between two segments of a market. The first survey is described as the 'donor survey' which is transferred to the second survey, the 'recipient survey'. The fusion process depends on statistical calculations which measure the similarities between the two surveys. When all similarities have been analysed, then the rest of the data stands alone for further analysis to establish its significance. Data fusion is only effective if the surveys can be matched or have been carried out using similar sampling and analysis techniques.

# Analysing data

Good analysis of data depends on good questionnaire design since unless the data collection method is well laid out, then it is likely to be difficult to analyse the data collected.

The basic method for analysis is a cross tabulation of analysis which cross analyses each question in the questionnaire with the key variables in the market – socio-economic classification, area of the country or whatever factor is being researched. But these are likely to provide 'top line' information and detailed understanding of the market or consumers' attitudes to the product being researched may not be evaluated in sufficient detail. More complex techniques start with multivariate techniques used in survey research and they relate to three different uses:

- **Developing a segmentation analysis.** Factor analysis is a technique which analyses the answers to a 'battery' of questions, whether they are attitude or image statements. It groups those questions which have been answered and links data that has similarities. Cluster analysis is a similar technique which groups respondents who answer questions in the same manner.

The data analysis therefore creates the segments that exist within the data.

- **Using a preference analysis.** Conjoint analysis is typically used to determine whether one factor is more important to a consumer than another. This might, for example, relate to package style compared with the size of a pack in which a product is packaged, analysing which type of pack a consumer prefers.

- **Applying complex forecasting techniques.** These are mainly multiple regression techniques which analyse the relationship between one dependent variable and a group of variables which are 'predictors'. The simplest form of the technique is time series analyses.

71

All of the above techniques are available to the numerate manager and those interested in applying computer packages. The most effective way of measuring results is to develop the data analysis into a graphic presentation. Even the non-numerate manager cannot fail to appreciate the results of a survey if they are clearly laid out in graphic format. Most computer software packages include a graphics package and all are easy to use for the non-technical computer user.

# Applying analysis techniques to decision making

Most surveys reveal that one sub-group has a greater preference for a product or is more active in a market than the rest of the defined consumers. It is therefore both logical and important to segment the market to gain a greater understanding of the opportunities for targeting by understanding the nature and characteristic of the target segment.

Segmentation measures which are most effective in measuring research survey results are the following:

- **Socio-economic classifications.** The characteristic of the consumer is described by sex, age and social class grading. The importance here is not just to analyse the information, but to make up groupings which have a significant meaning in sales and marketing terms. One such grouping would be a life-cycle analysis – early stage, family stage and late stage – relating the age of the consumer with likes and dislikes and how these change with age progression.

- **Geographic classifications.** Typical segmentation criteria that can be applied to any market. This has become more interesting through the 1980s as more detailed geodemographics systems have been developed. These will be covered later in this chapter.

- **Consumer behaviour analysis.** We saw earlier in the book the most effective way to analyse the market is to segment it according to current and potential customer or those consumers who are aware and not aware of the product or manufacturer. This behavioural analysis provides much more meaningful analyses than a basic socio-economic classification.

Analysing data has, in essence, become more difficult for the user as there are now so many different techniques available. The user has to decide what is needed. Careful and well-thought out use of the techniques will enable managers to make the data they need both relevant and actionable information.

73

# Computer techniques

There are some analysis techniques which are becoming very effective in the management of information and which managers are finding useful. Research and information is becoming more useful to them for planning and monitoring sales, marketing and communications as a result.

# Geodemographics

The most significant development of the application and use of existing data is geodemographics. The techniques of geodemographics take the information from the census data in any country and re-analyses it for any interesting application of the data that is available. For example, in 1993 the

Irish Trade Board completed an analysis of the census to identify the location of the Irish-born residents in the United Kingdom to plan direct marketing for Irish manufacturers and suppliers. Its most effective use is to provide research and marketing personnel with the means to both understand and target consumers effectively.

Geodemographics originated in the USA in the 1970s when the US Navy had experienced recruitment problems. The Navy took the US census data to identify large population concentrations of young males eligible for recruitment. Identifying them by the state, town and areas they live in, the US Navy developed promotional campaigns in the areas identified.

UK geodemographics date back to 1979 when a census-based geodemographics system was developed called ACORN (A Classification of Residential Neighbourhoods). The system has 38 neighbourhood types clustered into 11 specific groups. It is based on the assumption that people who live in similar areas – housing and surroundings – are likely to have similar behavioural, purchasing and lifestyle habits. Manufacturers and service companies can then target their products and services to the similar areas that have been identified.

The initial and successful application of the technique has been for the retail sector which has used it to define branch catchment areas, new site and re-location analysis, and target customer promotions for discount schemes and special offers. What is interesting about geodemographics is the trend analysis that it is now providing which measures the affluence of target customer types and how these change over a period of time.

Other very effective users of the geodemographic

classification systems have been the financial services sectors. Banks, building societies, insurance companies, investment advisers and stockbrokers have all used some aspect of the data for cross-selling and to analyse the areas around branch networks. An application for Acorn is the pinpoint analysis in the UK of the financial services sector's Financial Research Survey. The analysis is based on the findings of the financial survey, and it looks at the way people behave in terms of money – whether they have shares, bank accounts, investment trusts, pension funds, etc., – and uses this analysis to develop neighbourhood discriminators and characteristics.

One of the problems that now exists with regard to geodemographics is that there is a number of competing systems available, making the decision as to which one to use a complex one. The most significant development for the industry has been the advance in computer technology, allowing PC-based programs to do complete detailed and complex analyses. The development of PC-based geographic information systems (GIS) has been the most significant development, allowing data to be mapped and analysed visually. The more advanced companies in applying computer techniques merge the geodemographic data with their own internal information and other external data for customer and market modelling and profiling on their own marketing information systems.

75

The argument for geodemographic information relates to its accuracy and relevance to the user. The importance of lifestyle information from survey research is that it represents actual information on a specific product purchasing and consumption habit, relating the data to the consumer needs and changing trends in the market. But most of these surveys are representative sample surveys and the lifestyle data coverage, both in terms of its geography and socio-economic spread, will be limited to be representative of the population.

A geodemographic system will provide total representation as every household in the country returns a Census form to the Government. Various parts of the classification of this information are used for marketing purposes:

- owner occupancy provides important marketing factors, such as disposable income and negative equity
- multiple car ownership provides an indicator of the degree of affluence of the household
- ethnic origin is important for identifying niche markets and specialist sectors for specific products and services
- occupation of householders relates to their background, interests and buying habits
- mode of transport to work gives an indication of the household's mobility and needs in each part of the country
- socio-economic classification gives an important profile of consumer status and likely affluence.

When the above types of data are combined, then the ability of targeting products, markets and geographical or regional marketing campaigns is increased. Acorn itself has developed its services for specific targeting. Household Acorn provides direct marketers with the facility to understand and reach individual householders within a neighbourhood. Investor Acorn combines data on share ownership to target consumers who are more likely to spend on top of the range and luxury products. Arts Acorn combines data on people who attend arts events to help arts venues to target likely customers more effectively.

# Using geodemographics to grow your business

As the competitive environment of the 1990s continues, more and more marketing management will use geodemographics and lifestyle analyses. Geodemographics are effective if they are used in the marketing information system with other classification systems, such as the standard system for age, sex and social class. Geodemographics have strength in their use for understanding the characteristics of the market, using a postcode analysis, and giving precise and detailed targeting. Lifestyle analyses have become effective in direct marketing as they provide mailing lists of target consumers of 'like' characteristics.

77

The geodemographic systems that exist are:

- ACORN – a classification of Residential Neighbourhoods based on 38 neighbourhood clusters

- PiN – a more detailed system based on 60 neighbourhood types

- FiNPiN – a market specific classification developed on consumer research into consumers' financial activities from the Financial Research Survey (FRS) run by NOP

- Superprofiles – 36 target markets ranked by independent affluence and consumer indicators from both survey research and trade sales data

- MOSAIC – 57 neighbourhood types grouped into ten lifestyle groups

- Define – similar to MOSAIC but including a consumer financial analysis.

Lifestyle Databases build large databases sourced from 'lifestyle' questionnaires.

National Demographics and Lifestyles is based on ownership registration and other data. The data is usually used for tracking sales and monitoring customer satisfaction.

Computerised Marketing Technologies is based on data from the National Shoppers' Survey. It contains three to five million records and is used as a market sector mailing facility in segmented filed called Charity Bank, Media Bank, Finance Bank and CAR Bank.

International Communications & Data is a database of shareholders sourced from share registers.

These lifestyle databases are available to management through list rental services. The impact of their availability in the market has been to draw a very careful distinction between these systems and market research data. Lifestyle data provides the actual names of respondents for marketing, which under the Code of Conduct of the Market Research Industry contravenes the parts of the Code that provide reassurance of confidentiality when carrying out survey research. Use of these services therefore has to be defined carefully and where possible survey research and direct marketing should not overlap as a direct relationship of the analysis.

The main use of these classifications systems is for both identifying and profiling the customer base – where they are and who they are. Geodemographic profiles are profiles of the neighbourhood within which customers live. Profiling a customer database against a lifestyle analysis means the two databases have to be matched. Key applications given an address with a postcode, attaching a neighbourhood classification are:

- sales customers databases
- rented mailing lists of customer types
- door-to-door targeting for direct mail
- user and attitude research in certain neighbourhood types
- retail catchment area analysis
- sales territory analysis and allocation.

Geographical information systems are computer-based systems for storing and using information that can be related to specific locations or areas. In the context of geodemographics and lifestyle analyses, GIS are the delivery systems for reports and maps which the user might require.

79

Geodemographics will grow as more data becomes available and customised classifications are developed for market sector and product groups. These developments will relate to better door-to-door distribution and trade marketing for targeted localised marketing activity. GIS will stimulate this as they become the central operating and focal point of the marketing information system.

# Market mapping

It might sound rather obvious to a manager but there are benefits to market mapping in understanding the extent of the market the company is operating in and the performance of the company's products at all levels in the structure of the map. However, there are two definitions of market mapping and both have to be clearly identified to clarify how the maps are constructed and how the information they provide is used. What is important for both applications of market mapping is that management sees them as another addition to the marketing information in understanding either the success of the products the company sells in the market or how the customers can be classified into different target groups, which relate to how they appreciate or respond to the product benefits.

Managers use market maps as follows:

- To establish clearly all levels of the distribution network, define what they sell, identify sales at all levels and if mapped on a regular basis establish specific trends in the different types of distributor.

- To define the target customer by relating their attitudes to product benefits – what they like and what they dislike – with the consumer classifications that are used in the market.

  The most effective classifications are those that segment the customer base according to lifestyle or life preference classification – those that are descriptive of the habits, activities and interests of the consumer. Although these have been developed by advertising agencies in some markets and used as general descriptions, most companies need to analyse their own survey data to make this type of market analysis effective. Typical lifestyle classifications in the 1980s have developed terminology such as 'Yuppies', 'Dinkies' and other such descriptions of the type of consumer they are trying to describe. (A Yuppie is a Young up and coming Professional Person.)

Market mapping is the first stage in setting up the market information system. It helps managers to:

- define clearly the size and shape of their markets and those components that constitute the market

- determine how the various levels or components of the market in the map relate with each other

- specify each of the sales, marketing and communications methods that are based for effective selling at each part of the distribution network, and monitoring the success of these methods.

In the competitive markets of the 1990s market mapping is becoming even more important in understanding the structure and nature of the trends in each of the segments. It is also effective in helping to develop the more creative aspect of sales, marketing and communications planning, as it creates a better opportunity for communicating to the target market more in the context of their lifestyles and habits. The use of mapping is therefore effective for developing sales messages, strap lines for advertising and other communications, and also in identifying, establishing and developing brand strategies. Brand mapping is being used by consumer goods markets to stimulate purchase and develop consumer loyalty towards purchase and repurchase of brands. It is therefore an analysis technique which helps a manager to understand the market and the behaviour of the customer in the market much more clearly, increasing the chance of taking consumer-oriented decisions.

81

## CASE STUDY

### A Government Tourist Office – mapping the market to understand tourists' needs more clearly

The role of a Government Tourist Office is to define the market for attracting visitors to the country it represents among the travelling public of the country it is operating in. It has to develop a marketing campaign which promotes the country, its features, its travel facilities and all aspects of what makes it attractive to a leisure or business visitor.

Our case study concentrates on a European country promoting its facilities, attractions and tourist areas in the UK. This European country is advanced in culture and leisure facilities and is aware that it is not promoting itself effectively as the number of visitors to the country from the UK was not showing sufficient growth. As a result, it approached market research organisations to establish which companies could assist it in collecting information on the potential traveller, in making its advertising and promotional campaign more effective, and in persuading the potential traveller to travel to the country.

Two aspects of the market analysis were required. The number of travellers to the country had to be identified from government statistics to identify whether there was a growth or decline in the number visiting the country. In this instance the number was static and it indicated an opportunity for stimulation of an interested or loyal market. The second aspect was to define the profile of the market, but to establish the segmentation in terms of those who knew the country well and visited it frequently, those who knew it and stayed there on the way to other countries, and those who were not visiting it but could be persuaded to take a holiday there. The segmentation also had to take account of two other factors that were important for marketing the country as a destination. Leisure travel divides into travel for a 'short break', a visit that is less than four nights, and a 'vacation' visit that is four nights or more. There is also the 'additional' visit which can be taken with one of the other options if a person visits a country more than once a year. The other more complex part of the segmentation analysis was relative to the marketing of the regions of the country – could these be promoted competitively for their facilities and the types of vacation that they could offer – active or inactive – depending on consumers' interests and lifestyles? The choice included culture and the arts, leisure and the beach, eating and drinking fine foods and wine, or pursuing specific sports such as swimming, skiing, riding, water skiing, etc.

The project was divided into three stages: a qualitative phase through group discussions to understand how travellers select a leisure destination and why they would or would not visit the country being researched; a further qualitative evaluation of only those people who had travelled to the various regions of the country; a full market quantification through in-home interviews (400 travellers who had visited the country and 400 travellers who had not visited the country).

83

The staged project provided the user of the data with a number of benefits for building up the data collection and analysis by deciding what the data was saying in the context of market needs and how the Government Tourist Office would use the data. What was effective from the stages of the research was how the Tourist Office understood the attitudes of the traveller and potential traveller to the country. It became apparent from the qualitative analysis that there were little differences in age or socio-economic classifications as people would travel there for cheap short breaks, or also go there for their annual vacations. The analysis of the qualitative data implied that the attitude and image statements that were required, and had to be created from this analysis, needed to relate to the consumer needs for allocating their time when at their destination in the country.

These statements were added to the questionnaires for the two surveys of four hundred informants each. Initial analysis of these confirmed the issues identified in the qualitative research and also provided the ranking of their importance for including them in the promotion of the country. But as the lack of age and socio-economic segmentation was confirmed it became essential to make a more detailed and market-oriented analysis.

Two analyses were completed in sequence as they provided the information which was much more useful for promotional campaign planning. The factor analysis applied to the attitude and image batteries analysed the four hundred informants in each of the surveys into eight distinct groups. Review of these groups, relating them to the marketing strategy, gave the opportunity for them to be revised and reduced into five segments. These were identified as 'interested in European countries – "Mastrichophile"', 'interested in culture', 'interested in leisure and sports', 'interested in scenery and the countryside' and 'interested in the food and wines of the country'. The success of this analysis was effective for developing a series of themes for the promotional campaigns. On a regional basis this became even more effective as the priority for promoting the region became more logical for the different segments in relation to the facilities and activities of that region.

Experience also shows that if sufficient segments are created, such as the five segments for the Tourist Office, a further cluster analysis is likely to make the age and socio-economic classification relate to the market and help to use the data in strategic marketing planning. This was completed for the Tourist Office and it allowed the socio-economic and age analysis to be clustered into six important groups. Relating the factor and cluster analysis created some very useful maps of the five market segments, giving the Tourist Office a clear analysis of the nature of the target tourist and who should be promoted to in terms of socio-economic targeting.

# Analysis which is market oriented

The analysis of the data that is being collected should be thought about when planning the survey. It has a direct relationship with collecting interesting data and having information which can guide the user to taking effective decisions, such as who to target promotions to. A basic analysis is likely to provide a 'look at the target', but is not going to be sufficiently informative about market trends or the attitude of the product or service user. Turning uninteresting computer tabulations showing columns of statistics into graphical pictures of the target customers through market maps makes the data more relevant to the market in reality. Geodemographics and the application of the data in this analysis with data collected in your own survey is the research industry's interpretation of 'virtual reality', making the statistics as realistic as possible in the context of the customer base. When the application of this technique allows better sales, marketing and communications targeting, then the whole marketing process becomes more accurate through effective data analysis. Market mapping then allows the attitude and image of the target customer to be related to market classification and gives the manager a better opportunity to develop sales and marketing strategies which relate to their habits and lifestyles.

85

## *Hints for measuring the results*

- *Decide on the analysis at the research project planning stage.*

- *Where possible make the analysis meaningful and apply a statistical or analysis technique to your own results.*

- *Ensure that the data allows a manager to develop a useful market segmentation, by analysing the data into the largest groups of the consumers within the analysis.*

- *If a geodemographic analysis of the target market is completed it can have a direct effect on the structure and cost of any survey that is subsequently carried out. Knowing where the market is located, its size and profile can allow specific quota sampling to be used which is more precise and cost effective.*

- *Spend time relating the attitude and behaviour of the target customer to the data to create a market map. Once the initial data analysis has been completed through a factor and cluster analysis, it is easy to create a map on a spreadsheet or graphics package on a PC.*

# 5

# You have the information – now use it

## Introduction

**M**any managers think that when the research has been completed then the task of the research is finished. They have the information, they have read it and it should provide them with the answers they are looking for. But it is at this stage that many managers become dissatisfied, as they think that the information they have is not of use and even, to some managers, not of interest to them. This situation should not occur if the research has been well planned and discussed with regard to the issues being evaluated. If it is carried out efficiently with a questionnaire that covers all of the essential issues and has a computer analysis which provides all of the results and detail of the information that has been collected, then the research should provide the manager with all the information he/she needs.

A well-structured and informative project should facilitate a manager to use the information effectively. But when data is collected it is often presented without much thought and interpretation, and the key issues are not highlighted to the user. Reports are often prepared which mean a lot to those who have been directly involved in the project but, because they have been badly written, are ineffective as internal documents for other management. And what is also very characteristic of many market research houses is that the reports lack detailed recommendations and implications – i.e. all the issues that management should consider, discuss and implement as a result of collecting the information. Often this is because the research house is only an information provider. It is not sufficiently knowledgeable about the competitive decision making of interest to the research user.

Once the research has been completed it is essential that management recognise that there is a further stage of the project for deciding on the implications and using the decisions. Research becomes effective, as a guidance for setting objectives, developing strategies and implementing the right sales, marketing and communications methods. The skill in achieving this is to identify in a presentation or report the issues that have been confirmed. A manager should recognise whether he/she has learnt anything new about the product, market or problem being researched. The data which does provide the new information, and which needs detailed thought and interpretation, should be highlighted for effective implementation. If there are any aspects of the information which are not clear and which need to be evaluated further, additional analysis of the data or additional research may need to be carried out to provide the essential information. It could be that the questions that were designed for the research did not provide a useful analysis. It could be that the informants have misunderstood the question and therefore the answer is not relevant and cannot be used for good interpretation. Or it could be that the computer analysis is not detailed enough and the real results of these questions are still 'hidden' in the volume of data that has been collected.

Management needs to feel confident with the information it

collects to use it effectively. It needs to recognise the positive and negative issues that emerge and act on them appropriately. It also needs to realise that often a research project will highlight that certain issues need further research analysis. Although it may be that the managers have not been asked the correct questions, it is likely to relate more to the fact that the research has been successful in identifying issues and problems that had not been known already. It is therefore logical to research these before taking any further decisions about them.

# Presenting data effectively

The best way of presenting data effectively is to present the data before a report is written. The reasons for this relate to being able to understand the information that has been collected, and to being able to determine the initial implications of the research results. There are also a number of other benefits to making a presentation first:

- It assists in planning the extent of the interpretation – what is new information, what is old information and where similarities in the data have been identified. These similarities may relate to where certain types of informant have made similar comments or where the different types of informant have a strong opinion about issues all through the research analysis.

- It helps to define whether the research objectives have been met and how successful the project has been in providing more information than had been expected. If the objectives have not been met it gives managers an opportunity to explain what problems occurred in the research and what implications exist as a result.

- It helps to identify any problems with the data and, if those seeing the data for the first time do not understand it, provides an opportunity for clarification or for further computer analysis before the detailed report is written.

- It establishes the issues that have been confirmed in the research and, when it comes to writing the report, helps the report writers compile a document in a format and style that is acceptable to the reader. This is important for some companies from the point of view of the 'jargon' and 'language' used by management.

The experience of the author with managers who have little knowledge and exposure to presentations is that they like to have all the data presented to them, but in a very simplified format. They like to be guided through the statistics and shown the argument for the interpretation, how the implications relate to their research objectives and the decisions they have to take. They are hungry for the information but eager to understand the implications quickly.

The technological developments in the use of graphics in recent years have enabled large amounts of data to be presented in the shortest possible time. The range of software programs which now exist have helped to improve the way in which the results of a research project can be presented and interpreted. It has removed the situation of non-analytical managers peering at slides with a 'forest of numbers'. It now allows them to enjoy a presentation which has variety in the use of numbers, words, graphs and even pictures. The graphic delivery of research results has also helped research be seen, realised and applied by a wider range of managers than in the past.

When the presentation is finished the report can be prepared. This will focus on:

- the issues the management team agreed on during the presentation
- the interpretation of any special analyses that had been agreed as worthwhile during the presentation
- the production of a report which is acceptable and interesting to the management of the company.

The skill here will be to note the type of emphasis, phraseology and stated use of the information mentioned by the management in the presentation and to incorporate all of these in the report.

91

## Customising reports

A market research report should be a management document which does not just end up on the shelf for reference, but is used and referred to on a continual basis. One of our clients, with whom we have worked for five years on an annual trade survey, keeps his annual survey of the market in his brief case. He is a sales manager who deals with a wide range of contacts in the industry, in this instance the book publishing and retailing sector. The report provides a competitive analysis of the performance of his company in the trade sector and he says that he uses the research project – his 'bible' – to help develop the sales arguments in the meetings that he has with trade customers.

Many researchers believe that customising research reports is difficult unless there is an on-going relationship with the user of the research. Effectively, the researcher is saying that over a period of time he or she is getting used to what the research users want, and as a result, the researcher improves the way in which he/she writes the report. My belief is that this rather a 'lazy' way of preparing effective reports as every report that is written should be customised to the reader and the company which have commissioned the research project.

A good report, which is 'customised' for the reader, needs to have the following qualities:

- It needs to relate the research project to the current situation and trends in the market. This helps to make the findings of the research more relevant to the users, but particularly to those who are not directly involved in the project.

- It needs to explain which parts of the database have evaluated or answered issues originally laid out in the objectives of the project. This helps to relate how the findings of the research have proved or disproved a research hypothesis.

- It needs to summarise the positive findings so that they are brought to the attention of the reader to interpret and act on.

- It needs to summarise the negative findings so that the reader can decide what to do about them and take decisions which make them more positive.

- It should have a summary of the main findings at the beginning of the report – i.e. a section which highlights the content of the report and is easily digested by the reader;

- and, separate from the summary, it should have a recommendations section which takes the key findings and changes them into:

— action for managers to take

— issues managers might like to consider that relate to strategies and objectives the managers are involved with

— rationale for taking decisions based on the facts presented from the informants in the survey who are likely to be current or potential customers, users or buyers of the products or services made or offered by the company.

A good report is a short report. It is one which is written in the 'language' of the potential reader from the point of view of the jargon, terminology and industry-related information which the reader is used to. It is one which reports all the findings of the research clearly, gives management feedback on the problems and issues being researched and provides actions on which to take decisions.

93

# Identifying implications

The most interesting aspect of finishing a research project is reading the computer tables for the last time and checking that the report contains the best of the research findings. It is only at this point that the writer of the report is ready to decide on the implications and the recommendations that can be made. However, it is not the easiest part of the research-reporting process and identifying the implications effectively depends on the 'consultancy' skills of the researcher. Knowledge of the market and interpretation of the research findings in this context of market activity improves the recommendations that can be made.

Implications of the research project are only going to be relevant to the reader, and accepted and agreed with if the writer of the research report has:

- a clear understanding of the market or the product or service being offered to the market

- a good understanding of what the readers are looking for in the information that they have requested

- the ability to turn information into actions and to argue the rationale for these actions

- an understanding of what issues are involved in deciding on marketing, sales and communications strategies, and which aspects of the data in the report support the need for specifying these

- an understanding of the significance of the results of the research and what these imply.

What research report writers sometimes fail to do is to break down the constituent parts of the research findings so that they relate to the most important aspects which concern the reader. It is vital that a research report discusses:

- the marketing implications, highlighting implications on how the reader needs to take decisions on how to approach the market, and how to adopt the most effective competitive strategy for selling to the market

- the sales implications, detailing the sales methods, the sales structure, and the positioning that the sales team ought to adopt to persuade customers and potential customers to buy the products

- the communications implications, i.e. how the company

will project its image to the market and how it will use the 'terminology' of the market, as collected in the research, to develop the best themes, strap lines and promotional messages to communicate both the features and the benefits of the products or services being promoted.

The implications section of a report also ought to make reference to the relative sales, marketing and communications strategies compared with those of leading competitors. Without such an implication a company cannot establish whether the research results indicate a better, worse or same competitive positioning for the user of the research data.

A professional research report writer will also be in a position to indicate whether the research has covered all of the relevant issues, whether the research needs to be completed again to explore certain issues in more detail, or whether new research needs to be designed, set up and run to explore issues which have been identified from the initial research project.

95

## CASE STUDY

### A chartered surveyor – using a structured approach to implement research findings

Take the example of an established chartered surveyor. Traditionally a company concentrating on estate management and development, it had grown its residential and commercial property business in the 1980s and set up a specialist division to handle leisure and tourism developments. The company had not adopted any formal roles and marketing plan, but had depended on the property portfolio, advertising in key journals such as *Country Life*, and using public relations to the property journalists and leisure writers to maximise its communications effort.

As the boom in the property sector dwindled, the company increasingly came under competitive pressure. For the first time it appointed a Marketing Director who realised that the company required a central coordinating function to develop the appropriate marketing methods for each of the divisions. The new director adopted a planning procedure and took the opportunity of using specialist marketing consultants to set up a strategic marketing plan. He also initiated a review of the corporate image of the company, as development in this area had fallen behind that of the competition.

The consultancy obtained immediate agreement that any planning should be based on the attitudes of existing and potential clients, and on an assessment of the services of the chartered surveyors in relation to its main competitors. A 'perception' survey was set up among a series of target groups for each of the various divisions – these included recent customers, lapsed customers, non-customers, intermediaries, financial journalists and even competitors.

In-depth, semi-structured qualitative (attitude type) interviews with 22 clients were carried out, as was structured qualitative research by sending self-completion questions to 30 property media journalists. Following these initial evaluations quantitative research was also completed among the main client base, consisting of 1,000 self-completion questionnaires – 255 of these were returned.

In the quantitative (large-scale statistical) phase of the project the clients regarded the professional expertise of the company as high. The quality of the work was good and there was little criticism of standards – the level of services was considered to be on a par with other major competitors. The company was considered to have a high profile in leisure (the newest division), landed estates and up-market residential, with a low profile in the commercial sector. It was also seen to be poor in communicating with its client base, with a third of the informants saying that they were not aware that the firm had other divisions, apart from the one which they used. The majority of the clients wanted a more proactive approach to their business from the surveyor.

In contrast, the survey among the journalists showed that the surveyor had the lowest profile in the Press, indicating that the media had not appreciated the extent of the company and its operations.

In the quantitative phase, the clients were asked to rate the services of the company using 'attitude statements' which were drawn up to help the informant in the survey discriminate between the surveyor and its competitors. The surveyor's strengths are seen to be 'helpful staff', 'professionalism', 'personal service', 'confidentiality', and 'quality of work'.

97

The results of the perception survey highlighted that the surveyor needed to improve:

- its image in the marketplace as being a more proactive company
- its sales ability by providing clients with a more 'creative' approach to their requirements
- the ability of the professional staff – a training programme was initiated to increase their awareness towards marketing, and to improve their own sales skills
- its overall marketing approach – its emphasis on PR had not proven to be effective and it was clear that the company urgently needed to become more aggressive with its sales and marketing, improve its communications and become more 'competitive'.

The perception survey was useful as it helped the company see itself as clients saw it, and to focus and target its sales and marketing more effectively. However, when the results were presented to senior management they were concerned about its findings. Comments were made by the Board of Directors that included 'we cannot use this information as it disagrees with our view of the market', and 'senior and middle management will find it difficult to interpret this information'. What essentially the Board was saying was that they were not used to using and interpreting data. They were a sales-led company and were not analytical in their approach to management decision making.

The consultants responded aggressively but professionally in demonstrating to the Board that their 'ostrich' like approach would damage their competitive position in the market. They said rejection of the data would not allow them to take decisions from the clients' viewpoint and this could affect their overall competitive position. Their solution was to develop strategic planning sessions, which were designed to help the Board and managers not only understand the implications of the research, but also to undergo training in how to be more analytical and consider the clients' viewpoint.

Brainstorming sessions were held where groups of managers were asked to list out their decisions on how to implement the data, and to present their rationale for taking the decisions. The consultants undertook the same exercise and both groups then analysed each other's lists for the strengths and weaknesses of the decisions taken. When these activities had been completed the Board of the company agreed that they had been shortsighted in their original comments and recognised that they had invested in a research project that had been worthwhile and which all management could make good use of. The research and its implications had had an effect on the culture of the company and its use of information.

It is clear that traditional reporting methods for research would have been limited in this instance. Working with the management to interpret and implement the research achieved both acceptance and use of the data.

# Conclusion

When the research information is made available there is work to be done to make the data meaningful to the managers wanting to use it. It is important for management to become confident with the data so that it can learn new aspects about its customers.

A full presentation of the data before the report is written provides an opportunity to review the data and develop 'the database' on the implications of the data and on how the information will be used. It also provides a forum for bouncing ideas around and for doing further analysis to prove or disprove the issues being discussed.

99

The report on the research will include all the issues discussed at the research presentation. Because the issues have been discussed and debated, the report document represents the agreed research interpretation – i.e. the consensus view of the management team.

The implications help to specify the marketing methods and techniques which will allow a company to grow by improving consumer targeting. They become the 'benchmark' on which further research and analysis is completed. They also provide a standard against which the effectiveness of decisions taken can be monitored. In this way research becomes an effective tool for identifying where there are opportunities for growing the business. Once these are identified, it also becomes the monitoring mechanism of the potential growth areas, indicating whether they are providing new success or whether further financial, sales or marketing support is needed to make them successful.

## *Hints for Using the Information*

- *Develop reports which are interesting, relevant to the user and contain implications that make the research not just a piece of information, but something that can be acted on.*

- *Present the findings of the research before reporting on it as the presentation will help to check out the acceptability of the information and other issues that need further analysis.*

- *Use graphic and colour formats for the presentations as they will enhance the fast delivery of a large amount of information as well as help the audience to assimilate, understand and interpret the information effectively.*

- *Ensure that reports are 'customised' and that they are structured, focused and include detailed recommendations that relate to the user of the data and the reader of the report.*

- *Highlight the strengths and weaknesses of the research findings so that managers can review the positives and negatives to help them to improve and enhance their decision making.*

- *Provide detailed interpretation and sufficient information on the implications of the data to make the collection of the data worthwhile, rather than recognising it as just a piece of information.*

- *When analysing research take a 'step back' and decide what you really do not know about your customers.*

- *Develop a series of questions that need to be answered and which the research analysis has to review carefully.*

- *Determine what competitive measures are required so they can be extracted from the database.*

# 6

# Making sure that the customers are happy

## Introduction

One of the most interesting 'global' developments over the last eight years has been the interest in getting the customer viewpoint to verify attitudes to products and services. With innovation occurring more quickly and products becoming uniform in different markets around the world, customer service has become the focal point of effective marketing and communications.

Customer care monitoring has been the key growth area of the market research sector in recent years. The reasons for this include:

- market stagnation, with some sectors experiencing excess supply – many companies are therefore keen to keep their customer base and satisfy their customers in a way that their competitors are not able to do.

- higher consumer sophistication, leading to greater expectations for being satisfied, has developed the 'charter' culture for satisfaction

- increased management interest in total quality management (TQM) which takes care of the balance between the external and internal consumer and how good interaction between the two enhances good customer care.

# The rationale for customer monitoring

Some managers may feel that they know the 'pulse' of opinion of their customers. Regular visits from field sales staff, technical representatives or any staff member can keep the communications between the supplier and the customer clear and identify the strengths and weaknesses of the relationship. But this type of contact is not systematic in terms of an independent way of collecting information and it is prone to bias. Individuals are always interested in presenting the positive aspects of business relationships and any concern or dissatisfaction expressed by a customer is likely to be rationalised when reported back to senior management.

Independent objective customer analysis will provide meaningful feedback which can be tracked through trend analyses over time. Some companies which have regular research activities may believe that they are already collecting sufficient customer monitoring information through their survey research and customer research. But this is not quite the same as the specific role of customer care as it is important to construct a questionnaire which addresses two areas relating to the relationship with customers. Indeed, there is also a potential for confusion between general survey data and the customer care analysis, and a specific customer monitoring has to be planned, set up and analysed as a separate activity. The two areas which are effective for a customer care programme are:

■ assessing all elements of contact with the company – letters received, telephone contact, speed of dealing with enquiries, speed of delivery, etc.

- giving an evaluation of how well the customer believes the company has provided a good or bad product and service, and the degree to which they have been satisfied with the type of service provided.

An efficient and effective way of completing this analysis is to create 'attitude' statements, which describe the type of contact the customer may have had. 'Fast and efficient response to enquiries', 'clear invoicing', and 'solved my query very quickly', are all typical statements which the informants in the survey are asked to rate according to a bi-polar scale for Agree to Disagree. The overall assessment is taken from a question which describes their satisfaction, 'Overall how satisfied are you with the service provided by . . .'? Again this is rated on a bi-polar scale for Very Satisfied to Very Unsatisfied.

Where there is overlap between a customer monitoring programme and regular survey research there is the need to link the findings of the assessments of service and overall satisfaction with what is important or unimportant to the customer in relation to how the service is provided. There is nothing wrong with this, but it has to be taken as a rating in conjunction with the customer ratings, rather than completed as a rating in isolation.

## Uses for customer care monitoring

Management now has the opportunity of taking advantage of a series of new trends that have emerged for customer monitoring. These include:

- the focus on researching customer retention

- the growth of 'mystery shopping' – observation of how the customer is cared for (the virtual reality of customer monitoring) at the place of work and in the process of dealing with customers

- using the data results to provide an index which, if collected regularly, provides an indication of performance which all management can use as an indicator of their decision making

- calculating staff rewards and profit sharing based on the performance indices collected

- reporting customer care monitoring results in companies' annual reports.

There has also been a consolidation of an increasing trend in creating data where it did not already exist, but its contribution is to provide an additional indication of how effectively service is provided. Publishers researching bookshops' customers, industrial manufacturers researching the end-user market of the product that their components constitute, are all forms of customer care. It is getting good feedback from the user on how well the user is being looked after, and whether you are achieving this more effectively than your competition.

Customer care research is therefore an important technique for measuring performance, evaluating people and the services and the style of service they offer. It evaluates all aspects of service and how it is provided, such as standing in a line, and the way in which the service is delivered, such as the friendliness and courtesy of staff.

# Key guidelines

Management needs to be aware of key guidelines when making sure that customers are happy. These include:

- obtaining the commitment for all staff and management to collect, interpret and use the data as it is essentially data about how well they are doing

- accepting that a performance indicator is the focal point of the quality management programme, which 'drives' the customer monitoring

- planning carefully the questionnaire content and the specialist techniques for the data collection so that they are sensitive to all customer case issues

- analysing the data graphically so that the findings, trends and implications can be realised and interpreted quickly

- recognising that the trends that are identified may lead to a restructuring or redesigning of the project and questionnaire content as management realises the need for more precise feedback from customers, depending on how they view your performance.

105

## CASE STUDY

### A US airline – using research to provide an integrated monitoring system

Let us take the example of an international US airline which has developed the results of the customer care research into the corporate culture of the whole company. Delivery of bags at the carousel at the airport, waiting time for take off on the runway, reaching the gate on arrival at the destination airport, and schedule reliability are all presented monthly from the continuous customer satisfaction surveys. Competitive and internal on-board survey results are even presented to flight crews so that actionable market research is used by operating staff, financial staff and marketing staff to check how well the overall service is being received.

Decision makers are therefore involved in customer attitudinal data by seeing continuous data on customer attitudes. What is interesting about this airline is how it uses the data for quantifying trends. Typical management meetings of any company include viewing management financial data and hearing a manager say, 'We are five percent above the revenue plan'. Now companies can add other comments, as this airline does: 'Customer comments on our schedule reliability are five points above our goal'.

However, a company like this airline, which is 'customer led' in its decision making, has to distribute the information through the company carefully. The airline has created measurement techniques to make the 'intangible aspects of its service into tangibles'. The data extracted from on-board surveys is sampled in various languages. The surveys are run with two questionnaires. One asks about marketing topics, issues like ticket purchase decision, timing of travel and where the ticket was purchased, length of stay, the purpose of the trip, awareness of flight schedules, fares, etc. The other questionnaire is concerned with customer satisfaction. Passengers are asked to rate all aspects of the operation from reservations, flight check-in to on-board service and meals service. One per cent of flights are sampled within the US and 10 per cent internationally. Passengers have been asked to give their names and addresses. The zip code analysis is used with a geodemographic package which provides segmentation and demographic data as discussed in chapter 4.

This customer monitor has become very effective for quantifying the importance of different areas of the airline's operation by using factor and discriminant analysis of all the attributes and the degree to which they explain a customer's flight satisfaction. The airline has found that its customer satisfaction research has become more central to the business planning than other aspects of its marketing. This is because the management style is goal driven and is open to accepting and using quantified data.

# Conclusion

Customer care monitoring is likely to develop further in the future. Companies will become more interested in collecting data on customer retention and on customers who have lapsed. It will also be extended to understand how new customers' expectations are satisfied. There will also be a greater dependence on relating the findings of the research with all elements of the operations of the company. It will therefore help to assess how to improve market penetration, market shares, and the overall sales of the company.

A recent report from the Henley Centre and the Chartered Institute of Marketing stated:

> This more competitive environment will focus greater attention on the potential of existing customers. This will take the form of:
>
> – assessing lifetime values and thus the value of promoting loyalty
>
> – the ways of increasing the value of given customers through cross selling.

It is therefore extremely important that the marketing of a company is directed towards building loyalty among existing customers as the cost of replacing an existing customer with a new one can often be as high as tenfold.

In order to measure the success of the customer loyalty it is essential that trading and evaluation procedures are incorporated. Marketing needs to be monitored against objectives set by measuring changes in behaviour and attitude. The results of the tracking provide clear performance measures and information for future planning.

Customer monitoring programmes are making the techniques of survey research much more accessible to all levels of management – as high as Boards of organisations. They are exposing more managers to the analysis, interpretation and the effects of using external independent data. Management is therefore finding that new company systems are being created which help them to take customer-led decisions. Later in the book we will see the significance of trend analyses and how they impose on the long-term decisions that management take.

Trend analysis of customer monitoring programmes really does provide feedback on whether the right decisions are being taken. Good interpretation of these programmes proves that data can be used to ensure sales increase.

### *Hints on developing customer monitoring*

- *Gain agreement with all levels of management that customer monitoring feedback is to be used at management meetings to measure performance.*

- *Decide on the techniques to be used but ensure that sufficient numbers of interviews are carried out to represent **all** types or classifications of the customer.*

- *Use a definitive list of customers which provides for both users and buyers of your products and services to get a good comparison of* the type of customer and the contact he/she has with the company.

- Design the attitude statements carefully to measure all aspects of customer contact. Do not make the evaluation too exhaustive, but ensure it includes all aspects that can be assessed for good and bad performance.

- When you first set up the programme, design it bearing in mind what has to be assessed and measured in a 'trend' analysis.

- Keep the analysis of the information simple using graphic output so that the data can be widely used in the company.

- Decide on the feedback to the customers of the results of the customer monitoring. Publishing data in the annual report, newsletters and other company information is an important way of reassuring present customers and demonstrating to potential customers the quality and level of service.

# Tracking trends and changing decisions

## Introduction

So far in this book we have seen how to make good decisions by recognising that using information enhances the decision-making process. We have also established what is essential information to a manager: data that is available from internal systems and data that can be collected from internal research. There is, in addition a series of external research techniques which are more desirable to use because they yield good information that relates to sales, marketing and communications. We have realised, too, that there are important ways of analysing, presenting and reporting the data that make the research findings both actionable and effective.

What is also important for management is to understand how to work with these techniques to make use of research-led sales, marketing and communications in decision making. Effective research use and implementation has a direct relationship with being able to devise ways of setting strategies to expand company business. Those who have experienced the effective use of information to grow business have realised that it is not the research they have been doing, but the way they have been doing it that has resulted in making sure the research is effective. The key is to be able to use research to track trends, understand changes in the market and learn to review and change decisions based on the trends that have been identified.

Research can often be viewed as providing information as a 'snapshot' of the customers' opinions and the situation in the market. If a series of 'snapshots' are created through the research being completed on a regular basis, then the snapshots can be linked together and the findings of each stage interpreted. In fact, it is just like creating a movie with the frames of each 'take' or 'snapshot' providing a sequence which can be interpreted by management to monitor the effectiveness of the decisions they have taken between intervals. Unlike a movie, the sequence of the research may not have an ending or conclusion as it provides an on-going view of the situation. The 'epic' effect of the monitoring may have a direct influence on the nature of the decisions management take over a long period of time, because of the trends that are likely to emerge.

Management may also find that a practical and effective application of research techniques is to track trends in the delivery of customer service, as we have seen in the previous chapter. The 1990s are seeing an increase in the number of management teams using research in this way, which in itself is exposing traditional research techniques to higher levels of management in the company. Senior management are now more concerned about customer satisfaction and they are becoming more involved in designing research projects which are providing the benchmark data for customer monitors that will last over a period of many years.

Using research information to track trends is likely to have a direct effect on increasing sales and growing the business.

Understanding, tracking and monitoring your own success-es, failures, competitive positions, new products or commu-nications on a continuous basis will give an independent and objective way of improving decision making. If the analysis is used by all levels of management in a company, then it is not just using research as a management tool, it is proving that research can be used as the most fundamental way of devel-oping, running and implementing sales and marketing plans.

## Monitoring market shares

Most companies are proficient in monitoring market share, but few use techniques to do it in a systematic manner. Share monitoring is effective and is vital in:

- understanding if your sales are better in an increasing market, a static market or a declining market

- knowing which competitors are performing better and which are worse

- knowing which product categories are selling better or worse than those of your competitors

- identifying whether our own awareness in the market is better or worse than that of your competitors

- establishing if sales are particularly concentrated in a cus-tomer base, compared with competitors' sales concentra-tion.

Market share monitoring differs in a number of companies. Each of these needs to be discussed to determine how effec-tive it is for growing business. They are:

- Informal discussion and information exchange with competitors to 'check' how the company is performing compared with them.

Typically done at trade shows and exhibitions, this is a very unsystematic way of collecting market share data. It is also likely to be inaccurate depending, as it does, on estimates and indicators that are verbal 'hearsay' and, in some instances, on figures which one company may want its competitors to believe rather than reflect the real situation.

- Submitting data to a trade association or an independent organisation appointed by a group of companies in the same industry or sector to collect and disseminate the information collected.

113

This is a systematic method for collecting market share data and it is a way for competing companies, sensitive about using data with competitors' information, to become more analytical in their approach to decision making. As a method for sharing sales information it has to include the following:

- careful preparation of the questionnaire or a data sheet that is used to collect the information. It must have classifications for market and product sectors or categories which are used or are meaningful to each company carrying out the information exchange and share analysis. This has to be developed, discussed and agreed as it is unlikely that each company will have the same classifications

- the sales periods of the data being submitted must be the same for each company, otherwise there cannot be an effective comparison of the information

- the analysis must also be informative and provide information which can easily be interpreted.

Some market share information exchanges just take in the

data from all companies and then disseminate it without any further analysis. Say, for example, 54 insurance companies submit their monthly sales data of life insurance policies. These are listed in 23 different categories. The 54 entries are added for each of the 23 categories and the data printed on separate sheets. Twenty-three sheets are then issued showing entries numbered one to fifty-four, the numbers being the only identity given to the companies participating in this data exchange. Each company therefore gets back their own sales data and those of competitors, but only in the context of the sales trends in the product category.

Market share monitoring has become much easier as databases and spreadsheets have become the basic tool of management information systems in PCs. It also has changed some managements' attitudes to how quickly they need data and how current the information is. Sophisticated market share systems in the food and drink retailing sectors, automotive and automotive parts distribution sector, computer hardware and software sales are now set to provide information on a weekly basis. This required dedicated staff to both input and output the data. The volume of information that is generated is often too much and too detailed for a typically busy manager to read, interpret and act on. Most of this type of information is now not printed on computer output or spreadsheet tables, but in a graphic format which allows the quick interpretation of overall trends. This is more useful for a busy manager as it improves his/her ability to be able to take decisions.

## Developing tracking studies

In chapter 3 we discussed the need for developing customer

data to gain an understanding of the customer profile where customers are located and how their needs change. Tracking studies are essentially a means of collecting this customer data on a continuous basis. They are effective for monitoring all the sales, marketing or communications that companies are planning, have in progress or have completed.

Typically there are two types of tracking study:

One is a study which concentrates on the marketing effects of a communications campaign. Used mainly by companies that have heavy expenditure in advertising and promotions, data from these studies provide feedback on the effectiveness of the promotions in the total market. The traditional approach to this type of tracking study is to divide it into at least three stages. The initial stage is the 'pre-campaign' stage, which should include all the questions that the company has to ask to 'benchmark' the trends in the tracking study. Benchmarking means asking the questions in this initial phase and then repeating the same questions in the subsequent phases to identify the changes.

115

The 'pre-campaign' stage needs to establish what is the market that the communications **usually** reaches, what is the awareness level of the company investing in the communications, how this awareness level relates to that of competitors' and what recall exists for any communications. As this phase of the research typically takes place before a communications campaign is initiated, the data will provide good information on all of the above except for recall of the communications.

What is important, and is sometimes forgotten, is the need to analyse this benchmark data to interpret it and understand the implications of what it is saying. The reason for this is to make the research effective and understand the market's attitudes and reactions to the up-coming communications, so it can be used effectively.

Analysis of this initial phase is likely to help to define questions that could be added to the subsequent phases. Failure to complete this analysis at the first stage could mean that later stages do not contain the right question content which helps to collect data on whether company communications are causing target consumers to react or change their attitudes.

The second and any subsequent stages, phased in when communications are transmitted to the current and/or the potential market, should include the original stage one questions, otherwise the changes, drift and trends cannot be monitored. However, additional questions should be added to allow for sufficient evaluation of the effects of the communications. It is particularly important to assess the visuals of the communications to identify what is liked and disliked. Equally, information on the content, the copy or the words, the slogan or jingles and the strap lines is going to provide a better understanding of whether the communications are consumer oriented and effective from the point of view of obtaining customer loyalty and increasing sales.

The second type of tracking study, which is essentially to gain understanding of the users and buyers and their needs and buying requirements, needs to be on a regular basis. 'Regular' has to be defined according to the dynamics of the market sector in which the reader's own products and services exist. The food, computer, financial services and publishing sectors need such a study annually. Printing machinery, agricultural machinery or any 'minority' market is likely only to need data every other year. However, the content of this type of tracking study ought to be specified carefully. The structure of the questions should be reviewed in the context of the reader's own product group and industry structure. The questions should relate to the following headings:

- Classification of the market. In consumer markets this should be age, sex, social class, income and any other factors that are important for classifying the market, such as leisure and 'lifestyle' factors. In industrial markets this should be type of company, turnover, profitability, number of employees and any other characteristics that need to be classified.

117

- Definition of who are owners and non-owners, users and non-users, and how these target markets classify into 'heavy' or very regular users or buyers, 'medium' or fairly frequent users or buyers, and 'light', infrequent users or buyers.

- How much is paid for the products or services.

- How much is bought/used of the products or services.

- Where the products or services are bought or used and where buyers/users prefer to buy or use the products and services.

- Attitudes to the products or services (rated by attitude statements, phrased in the context of factors important to consumers, or how they tend to buy or decide to buy products).

- Media used to promote products or services.

Then the questionnaire should carry any other questions relating to new product development, and of course the communications development, and the communications campaign being evaluated. This is also another area where a badly designed questionnaire will not give the best feedback. Many managers forget to explore the reasons for the opinions given and it is these that provide the key to establishing whether a communications strategy needs to be refocused or elements of it changed or improved.

The following provides the guidelines to what should be included in the communications section of the questionnaire:

- awareness of the company, product or service (unprompted)

- awareness of the campaign (unprompted)
- awareness of the company, product or service (prompted)
- awareness of the campaign (prompted)
- what is liked about the campaign and why
- what is disliked about the campaign and why
- what is liked about the theme and why
- what is disliked about the theme and why.

If the communication medium is a newspaper advertisement:

- what was recalled about the copy of the advertisement
- how the advertisement caused the person seeing it to change his/her attitude towards the company, product or service.

If the communication medium is a TV or radio advertisement:

- what was liked or disliked about the visual or audio part of the campaign

- what was liked or disliked about the 'jingle', voice over and content of the advertisement

- how the advertisement caused the person seeing it to change his/her attitude towards the company, products or service.

Analysis of all of this information will not only identify the successes and failures of a communications campaign, it will also help to focus on where future campaigns can relate more specifically to the target market. Increasing the target market will, of course, lead to a growth in business.

## Using key data to take decisions     119

The research sector is full of technical experts, academics and practitioners who are very keen to talk about how research is done and what the technical strengths and weaknesses of the research are. What is important is to use this 'focus of excellence' to ensure that the research helps decision-taking. As there are so many techniques available, it is sometimes difficult to decide which to use.

A manager who is somewhat confused about the plethora of advice and guidance available has to organise himself/herself to know what to use. Earlier in the book we mentioned to the managers who do not think that research is of any use to them, because they have not thought about or discussed with colleagues what information is needed. The key to using data to take decisions is to list out:

- facts that you know about the market or the customers, which you need corroborated or confirmed as issues which then are not likely to be disputed or evaluated any further

- information that you recognise you do not have or data which clearly will help to take decisions which have not been taken because of uncertainty.

Experience shows that managers who do this benefit from thinking through systematically what data they could use. Most of them recognise that they have a vast amount of experience, preconceptions and prejudices, but few hard facts on which to base customer-led decisions. The result of this can be summarised into a number of different sets of data which become more central to the decision-making process. They are:

120

- statistics on the size of the market and the strata sizes within the sector
- data on the structure of the market in the context of suppliers and user industries
- information on the market trends
- statistics on the share of the market the company commands and how this relates to competitors' shares
- user, buyer and potential customer data on the image of the company
- independent assessment of marketing methods used by the company and how competitors' methods differ
- independent assessment of the sales methods and an evaluation of their effectiveness
- information on the effectiveness of distribution methods and how to stimulate them for their effectiveness
- customer assessment of the acceptability of product shipment and packaging
- statistics on the profitability of the product portfolio

- statistics on the costs and pricing
- customer assessment of the products and what they like and dislike about them
- customer evaluation of the effectiveness of the services of the company
- use, storage, dissemination of industry data and how this adds to the intelligence of the company
- statistics on non-domestic markets for all of the above
- survey research information on reaction to new products and product concepts being developed
- systematic analysis through survey research of competitive activity
- customer data on the demand for products, and
- regular survey research data on users' attitudes and behaviour, and assessment of the image of the company.

121

Many organisations are staffed at a high level by managers who only understand marketing as the selling function. They are concerned with the optimum price for the product they make with the most cost-effective production. Data such as the 19 points listed above does not feature in their day-to-day decision making. Reviewing this list will clearly show that their decisions are not market led and comparative to other suppliers. The most important aspect they lack is the monitoring technique and advantage of using market research effectively.

## CASE STUDY

### A food casing company – using research to track trends

Tracking trends depends on the product and the market and the structure and characteristics of that market. The food casing sector provides a good example of why trend information becomes not just essential in understanding how to grow business, but important in knowing how to respond to overall marketing activity.

Food casings are supplied to food manufacturers to make the end product. Food casing manufacturers are therefore dependent on the success of the sales and marketing activity of the food manufacturer. Indeed, they are essentially removed from the real consumer – the buyer of the end product that is constituted from all the food and casings.

Concerned about forecasting the market to maintain good customer relations for existing customers and also to devise ways in which to develop and increase the market, the food casing supplier decided to set up and run a market research programme. The company's rationale for doing this was to 'get closer' to the market to examine the trends and market characteristics of the end-user market as this has a direct impact on how the manufacturer can maintain and increase sales. The sales and marketing management realised that they could not make market-led decisions without any independent data which could help them to convince their own customers about consumer preference for their products and also to identify emerging trends in the market. What was interesting about this company was its concern to develop a programme which could be updated regularly and which could provide an 'early warning' system by tracking trends and providing an effective monitoring system to measure the decisions they had taken. The marketing information system that was created by this company included the following:

- **Analysing the company's sales statistics to determine market performance.** Three years' data was analysed in the computer and a trend analysis created. New sales statistics were then added to this annually and quickly a monitoring system was created. The company wanted to use this data as a predictor of market performance. The sales force had estimates of competitors' sales and this was added into the computer analysis. Additional data on economic growth and other market influences were also included and a 'market model' was created.

- **Developing annual survey research, identifying consumer preferences for the company's products versus competitors' products.** Regular product tests were completed to track consumer preferences for the food casings, compared with the competitors' products. This data was analysed and prepared in a graphic format which showed simply the percentage of consumers in the market that preferred the casings to competitors' products. This information was given to the sales representatives so that it could be shown to customers and potential customers as objective, independent data proving why their product should be bought and used to manufacture the end product. As it was tracked over a period of time, the data became even more convincing in demonstrating customer loyalty and product performance compared with varying competitor product quality.

- **Setting up a user and attitude survey which was then repeated every other year among a representative sample of the population of consumers in the total market.** This research project included all elements of market analysis and consumer classification. It was designed to provide all the background information on the user and the buyer of the products which included the food casings. The data provided information on the trends of the size of the market, the number of consumers paying for the product and how much they paid. It also gave a competitive

123

overview of which of the end-user products were bought, who was buying them and an evaluation of their attitudes to products that were introduced to the market. The data was also analysed in a graphic format and used in discussions with customers and for presentations at customer conferences. This provided their customers with more detailed knowledge of their own customers – the consumer, which helped both the casing supplier and food manufacturer to understand market trends and the customers' needs more clearly.

Research for this company was not just about providing essential information for market and product planning. It became the means of convincing customers that it had a good knowledge of the market. This also allowed the casing supplier to use independent and objective data to persuade customers to buy its products and thus helped the company directly to grow its business. It was also using independent objective customer data – product users and buyers – to inform its own customers – the shops – on what opportunities existed to grow the market, and as a result their business, with their customers.

# Developing trend data

Research is not worthwhile unless it makes a contribution to decision making. Its contribution comes when it provides new and additional data which influences management thinking.

Involvement in research is the manager's chance to play a role, just as a writer of a play or a movie script has to define the roles of an actor. The writer will decide on the theme or purpose of the movie. Characters are created to communicate the writer's message. The plot will test out the theme and the purpose with scenes that build up the overall picture of the underlying reason for the script. Taken together, in sequence, the scenes form a logical delivery of the movie and allow the person watching to learn something. The movie-goer will leave the theatre or the movie understanding a subject in more detail.

Research fulfils the same function for the manager as a play or a movie for the script writer. The manager has to set out the theme or purpose of doing the research. The information that he or she defines that is needed is likely to prove or disprove this theme, depending on the answers of those who are interviewed. The questionnaire, if constructed carefully, in sections which relate to various aspects of the overall purpose, will help to build a picture of the issues that relate to the theme. The analysis, presentation and reporting of the data will help the managers to understand what they have learnt from the research.

125

The important point for a manager to realise is that if the above is achieved then, just as a movie, there is a beginning, a middle and an end to a research project. But a movie with frames missing is disjointed and is unable to communicate the theme effectively – the viewer will not know the whole plot and will not realise the sequence of the message. A research project is also similar to this. Unless the research is planned over a series of projects relating to the market, then the results are unlikely to deliver the right message. It is therefore important to develop trend data, to understand the overall implications of your decision making and use the trend information that is emerging to influence and eventually direct your decision making.

The benefit of developing trend information is to create a real or detailed understanding of the company, its products and services in the market, its competitive positioning and monitoring the effectiveness of its sales, marketing and communications. None of these is going to be appreciated if research is completed on an *ad-hoc* 'one-off' approach. The snapshot is like one frame of the movie – it only gives an impression of the theme, the situation of the plot, part of the communications at one particular time. Companies who have realised the benefits of trend data say that:

- the trends give them a better long-term perspective of the decisions they have taken, helping to focus on the key decisions for the future

- it is easier to monitor the reactions of the target market and identify more clearly where improved targeting is needed

- information on the effectiveness of the sales, marketing and communications strategies over a long period helps managers to allocate funds more effectively in whichever department, whether it is sales, marketing or communications

- the research becomes a better investment as it becomes the monitoring tool and is the 'early warning system' for making corrective competitive action or identifying new market or product opportunities

- highlights when additional 'problem solving' or 'issue evaluating' information is needed and also makes its contribution in helping to design more relevant and more specific *ad hoc* research.

Trend data helps to monitor market sizes and the performance of the company in the marketplace. Regular use of attitude and image statements in attitude and image batteries that are not changed over the long period of the research provides the means of monitoring the total presence of the company in the market. The sensitivity of these statements is so precise in monitoring attitudes, motivations and buying habits that long-term customer monitoring programmes depend on the effectiveness of this technique. Trend data therefore gives the company total performance feedback, establishing whether it is taking the most effective decisions to ensure that the company grows.

# Conclusion

Market research is a marketing tool and management discipline which is underestimated for its contribution to decision making. Improving knowledge of the market will help to anticipate market or customer needs and allow the company to react before any changes occur to these in the normal course of business. Monitoring the effectiveness of the marketing methods used and evaluating them over a long period of time, research makes a definitive contribution to the decision-making process.

127

Regular and effective feedback, providing good knowledge and information, has to have a priority over 'guesstimating' and assuming without the relevant facts. Data and information help a manager to get closer to the market and understand why a customer wants a product, what influences the customer to buy it, and how much the customer is prepared to pay. Knowing this from independent data is likely to improve the decisions that a manager takes and have a direct effect on business growth as the company becomes 'consumer focused'. Growing the business becomes easier as known customer needs become opportunities more easily satisfied – success becomes more guaranteed.

## *Hints on tracking trends and changing decisions*

- *Develop your own 'movie' of the market in which you operate by agreeing what data is essential to track trends.*

- *Use benchmark data at management meetings to identify the extent to which company activities have changed. Tracking trends from benchmark information will help to influence the customer oriented decisions that can be taken.*

- *Recognise the need for measuring market performance and, without talking about confidential information, approach competitors to set up a market share monitor. They will find it beneficial if you approach them in the right way, informing them that they will be able to identify your share of the market and how it compares with their share.*

- *Integrate the research programme into your sales and marketing planning. This will ensure that you build in the necessary 'pre-campaign' and 'post campaign' evaluations and provide you with continuous feedback.*

- *Plot the trends on colour graphics as this will aid the interpretation of information, and therefore aid decision-making in the long term.*

# 8

# Getting the most out of business relationships with research companies

## Introduction

**M**any companies do not have research specialists as employees and have little resources for completing a professional research survey. Therefore, there are many who contact research companies for advice, guidance, research management and interpretation. But a manager who is not used to doing this or has done it and has not been satisfied with the outcome of the project or business relationship is in need of guidelines, as to the strengths and weaknesses of working with other companies. Their experience of the market and their understanding of your competitive positioning in the sector will help the focus on product and service opportunities for growing the business.

Worldwide there are some 2,500 officially registered research companies, identified as professional research organisations as opposed to management consultants. Each has experience in various markets, specialist resources and portfolios of clients in different industry sectors. Some specialise in personal interviewing, others in telephone interviewing, others in data analysis and computing. For those who are not familiar with any of these aspects of research, it is essential to get referral as to the details of the companies and their services. The Market Research Society in the UK, the American Marketing Association in the US and ESOMAR in Amsterdam all publish international directories of research companies by industrial sector of their experience.

## Commissioning research companies

There are essentially three types of situation that a manager might find himself/herself in when deciding on developing a business relationship with a research company.

- *No knowledge, experience or previous business relationships with a research company.* In such a situation as this, it is advisable for a manufacturer or service provider to select at least three organisations to contact. These organisations should be identified by the suitability of their resources and experience. Each of these would then be asked to submit formal proposals and the most appropriate selected to complete the project.

- *Knowledge of research but a need for external resources as little in-house skill for doing the research.* In such a situation as this, evaluation of potential companies might be on an informal basis. Asking three organisations about what they do in your particular area of interest would ascertain the relevance of their experience and probably add to your understanding of what could be achieved. It is likely that at least two companies will be invited to submit formal proposals for competitive pricing and methodology.

- *Dedicated to research and in need of developing the research programme particularly for continuous surveys, tracking surveys and customer monitoring, with or without professional research skills.* It is likely that this manager will have worked with a number of research companies and will know exactly which one he/she wants to work with for a long-term programme. He/she may approach another company to check the research pricing, but is more than certain to select the first company for their knowledge of each other's activities and needs, *modus operandi* and involvement in their presenting and reporting process. After a period of time, long-term business relationships are developed.

131

# Qualifications of suppliers

Market research is a specialised management tool, as specialised as public relations, advertising development, campaign planning and computer systems development. Any company offering market research needs to prove some factors to ensure that they are able to provide the support and guidance that is required. You need to know whether:

- there is good knowledge among the personnel in the company of your market, product or service
- they have experience of researching the type of projects that relate to your research requirement or marketing or sales problem
- the company has the resources and skills necessary to complete the work you require
- the organisation is a member of a professional association or institute and what quality control procedures and reas-

surances this provides for the collection of the data and its reporting for professional independent research analysis.

Some managers use their advertising agencies for advice and for implementing some research activities. The four points above apply to their experience in completing research which is likely to be oriented towards developing creative communications only, and does not provide the breadth of experience that may be required for evaluating sales and marketing problems.

Many research organisations find it difficult to communicate or sell their experience. They confuse protecting the confidentiality of the clients they have worked for and the projects they have worked on, which they have to honour under research industry codes of conduct, with describing their knowledge and providing good advice. Managers evaluating companies need to look for those companies whose written materials and verbal communications add to their understanding and knowledge of the subject being researched. Comments such as, 'Have you thought of. . .', 'When we last researched this area we found. . .', 'The implications of what you are interested in doing are. . .', 'I would advise the project is carried out by. . .', are all indicating a specific experience and knowledge to draw on and work with. Their skills are likely to complement your own knowledge and skills of marketing in your sector.

Other important factors for evaluating the service of the company that you might want to select to assist in your research project are their interest, experience and capability for making recommendations and listing actionable issues that may need further discussion within your own company.

They need to be able to talk about how the results of research have been used by other companies they have worked with.

Many research companies are just 'information houses' and they do not see it as their role to provide advice and guidance. However, the competitiveness of the research industry is such that more and more companies are realising that they need to help the information user to use the data. Those that are interested in doing this also have to be evaluated for their experience in providing this service.

There is a difference between a research company that uses the summary of the key findings as its list of recommendations and the company which adds to the summary at least six points which relate to sales, marketing or communications actions which management can discuss and act on. It is important to be aware and to be sure that the independent advice on the interpretation of the data relates to the initial objectives of the project and answers any problems that were highlighted as topics or issues to be evaluated.

133

## A short brief is not a good brief

An important part of developing and establishing a good business relationship is for you, as a manager, to communicate clearly why you require an external company to provide you with support and to describe what support you believe you need. The experienced researcher knows that a short brief is a bad brief as it is unlikely to describe what is required. It is also likely to reflect poor knowledge of doing research and confusion on the part of the commissioning company, as the brief is unlikely to have been discussed internally as to what can be achieved by the research. An ill thought out brief can also lead to developing a research project which is inadequately structured and thus results in providing information which is not relevant or conclusions that are unrealistic to the market conditions, structure of the company or planned marketing activity.

# Example of a 'brief' brief

An example of a 'brief' brief is shown below (p. 142). It is not specific enough as it does not:

- provide a definition of the objectives of the project

- specify what are the purposes of each of the parts of the project
- specify clearly all elements of the target market to be researched
- specify in which countries the research should be completed
- indicate the research hypothesis, information needs or objectives of using the data.

Developing a good brief also ensures that the research involves all management in the project and gives them the opportunity of thinking through why they need data, and how they are going to use it.

I have attended many presentations which have been to a large management group and a member of the team has queried the research or phraseology of a question. Usually they are people who have not been consulted about the project and who have not had a chance to think about the information and the interpretations and absorption of the facts being presented. I have also seen situations where someone has become quite objectionable about the findings of the research analysis and has very noisily disrupted the meeting. Usually these are managers who have been invited into the meeting five minutes before it started and they have not been briefed on the meeting, the purpose of the research or what information has been collected.

## Clarity and detail get good results

Some managers take the view that a research agency should be able to provide them with all the support they need without much in the way of explanations, as they are thought to be 'experts' on the market. This is a naive view as the research company cannot envisage the internal political situations of a commissioning company, marketing plans that are being discussed or ideas that need to be tested out.

Other managers say that they do not participate in market research because when they have done so in the past they have not learnt from it and anything that has emerged from the research they already knew. It is these managers who have not thought about the research and have not prepared a clear and detailed brief.

## Example of a good brief

An example of a good brief is shown below (pp. 143–144). The key constituents of a good brief are:

- an introduction, giving the reasons for the project
- a review of the sales, marketing or communications issues and the 'research hypothesis' and how it relates with this situation

- details of the target market to be researched and whether the company will provide the sample or specifications for the research company to work on when completing the sample for the interview

- any specific information requirements and areas that need detailed probing or analysis

- the schedule that is needed for the publication of results

- the budget and financial specifications for the business relationship

- any data or company information that is required to illustrate the brief and what is contained in it.

This approach to developing the business relationship with the researchers is advantageous to any manager using it. If comparisons between research companies have to be made, then the parameters have been specified and a judgment on the best company to use can be taken comparatively. If a busy manager already knows which research company to use, then the document is a detailed briefing which lays out the way in which the research management is to be completed and all members of the team are clear as to what can be achieved.

The final commitment to the business relationship has to come from the research company which is proposing to do the project. They must layout how they will organise the project and how they will deliver the requirements to the commissioning company.

## Quality proposal documents from suppliers

Just as there are good and bad briefs, equally there are good and bad proposals from researchers. What is different about the proposal documents is that a comparative analysis of the way in which they are written shows whether the company has the right experience to do the research.

## Example of a bad proposal

A bad proposal, as shown on pages 145–47, is one that is not 'tailor made' to the commissioning company's needs as identified in the brief. It is likely to be too brief, not provide sufficient information of what happens in the project, when it happens and whether there is a perception of where problems might emerge. It might give details of a specific research service the research company runs, but it might not relate to the commissioning company why this service is appropriate for the project that is required. It might contain too many of the following phrases which essentially indicate that the brief has not been thought through and that the company does not have the right experience to do the work. 'Until we have discussed. . .', 'It is not clear. . .', 'We cannot comment on. . .' This is not fantasy, but an account of what can be seen in reality. Such a situation directly affects the quality of the project which is carried out and the conclusions that are made when the research in finished.

137

## Example of a good proposal

A good proposal is one that has the following characteristics as shown on pages 148–55. It has an introduction which not only acknowledges the content of the brief that has been provided, but also details additional information on the market, product, communications. This helps to show the commissioning company that the research company knows the market. Some research agencies call this section a 'discussion' but I always find it difficult to see how one can have a discussion with a written document. There is seldom any dialogue in it which might illustrate that it is a discussion.

The proposal should state the rationale and the objectives of the project. Specific objectives can be listed in addition to this to indicate what can be achieved, particularly illustrating aspects of the service the company wants to provide – for example, 'to provide sales, marketing and communications recommendations'. It must also state the research method – why it has been proposed, the implications of using it, a description of what it is and issues that relate to the success of using it. This section should also contain:

- any advice gained from the experience of the research company doing similar projects

- details of the sample and sampling method and any problems associated with this initial part of the project

- perceived problems or areas for discussion with alternative solutions to inform management and help them to decide what to do.

Details of the fees and expenses and the terms and conditions of doing business with the commissioning company must be included in the proposal. The company should also state why it believes it is the right one to do the work, and provide details of previous experience and the client portfolio of the company. Finally, the proposal should include any other data or supporting information that the company believes is worth stating in the proposal document.

A well written proposal is likely to get managers 'nodding' in agreement while reading it. It also should be a document that the manager can pass around to other colleagues as it should be self-explanatory .

# Conclusion

Unless your company employs marketing research specialists who can run all elements of a market research project with your own company's resources, it will be necessary to use independent research companies. These organisations need to be selected for their experience and become additional to the sales and marketing planning activities – the personnel have to perform like the research manager, even though they are employed to support your company on a project basis.

139

However, when an effective business relationship is developed it can be beneficial to work with one or a selection of companies on a longer-term basis and even pay a retainer fee for exclusive commitment to your company and your sales and marketing plan. Achieving a constructive business relationship depends on being clear and cooperative in the conduct of the relationship. The mechanics of the project and whether the resources and facilities of the supporting company are less important than the research company's understanding of the market and its ability to interpret the sales and marketing implications of the research results. Good working relationships with research suppliers will help to ensure that good quality research results are provided. If the business relationship between your company and the research supplier is developed then the research supplier is likely to find it motivating to help your busines to grow.

### Hints on getting the most out of business relationships with research companies

■ Contact your own industry specialist to get a quality service complementing your own experience and market knowledge. If uncertain of who concentrates on your sector, contact the professional association and get a list of companies who claim your sector experience.

■ Check the research experience of the company you want to work with carefully. Do not select the company because it claims to have completed a lot of work in your sector unless you feel the experience of the company adds to the work and project tasks that your team is working on.

■ A research supplier who is not prepared to give advice and guidance on the results and the implications of the research could very well give you statistics you already have. A company that is interested in giving you advice and recommendations will approach the project in an analytical way, as you would, and therefore is likely to help to improve the project design. The result of this will be agreement on information that will aid certain decisions and the research company will be able to make their own interpretation of how the data affects these decisions.

■ Write a clear brief as you would be expected to be briefed. Do not make it a 'brief' brief.

■ Think carefully about who is going to be using the data. Ensure that they are involved in the project planning and implementation. This will help to avoid misunderstandings and bad briefing.

■ Evaluate research company proposals carefully. A good proposal is one which includes comments such as 'in our experience. . .', 'our knowledge of researching this sector encourages us to advise. . .', etc.

■ Write letters confirming all conversations in planning and imple-

*menting projects. Research suppliers are busy organisations and unless your requirements are detailed on paper there is a danger that a point in a telephone conversation could be forgotten until it is too late.*

■ *Recognise that if your requirements change at any time during the project, it is likely to change the business relationship. New ideas and new issues to be evaluated may not be included in the project easily. They may affect the costs and timing of the research and imposing them on the original relationship may have an impact on the quality of the project.*

■ *Try to develop a close working relationship with the supplier. If you tell the supplier everything about your requirements and brief them well you will get quality research and relevant and actionable results. Research companies are not 'soothsayers' and do not employ magicians. They are only going to produce a surprise out of the hat if you do exploratory customer research which reveals information you do not already have.*

141

142

## A 'BRIEF' BRIEF

### Introduction

Brieffacts Ltd. will be commissioning a large amount of work aimed at continuing the support of its products and services. The work will fall into the following areas:

- point of sales materials
- training materials
- advertising support
- sales incentive campaigns
- pricing strategies
- distribution development
- new product development.

In addition the company is interested in looking to develop its profile in the retail sector. Below are some of the identified issues that are relevant:

- branding of products for each target market
- database management for communicating with existing and potential customers
- market research, identifying perceived weaknesses and strengths and then actioning plans to respond to the findings.

I would therefore like to invite you to present your ideas on how you can add value to our decision making. An important part of the presentation will be information on your quality standards, and how they add to the quality of the project.

The proposals must be presented ten days from receipt of this brief.

# A GOOD BRIEF

## Introduction

Specific Facts Ltd. is proposing to carry out a customer confidence survey among their trade, consumer and business and professional customers. The purpose of this survey is to evaluate customer satisfaction relating to the company and the products. This is particularly important as the company has decided to launch a series of new products in what is essentially a very competitive market. It therefore wants to ensure that its current customers remain loyal and committed to the company, its products and services.

This research survey is being put out to tender and you are invited to present an outline of how the survey would be approached, giving details of experience, methodology, timings and fees and who will manage the project.

## Methodology

The survey is to be carried out by telephone interviews as the number of questions is relatively small and the questionnaire will contain both pre-coded and open-ended questions. The majority of it will involve attribute ratings on products and services.

## Sample

Specific Facts Ltd. has 60,000 customers and all these are listed in a name and address computerised marketing information system. This list has been segmented by user type

143

and geographic area to ensure that it is representative of the different types of customer.

## Topic areas for research

The key areas of information that will help the company to determine its customer service strategy are:

- contact with the company
- evaluation of accessibility to the company
- speed of problem solving
- speed of responsiveness
- quality of communications
- assessment of products
- attitudes to:
  - technical support
  - price
  - promotions
  - delivery
  - problem solving.

## Timing

The project will be commissioned in July 1994 and has to be completed for a customer conference presentation to all the company's customers in September 1994.

# A BRIEF PROPOSAL

## Introduction

Brief Proposal Ltd. have been asked to provide a proposal for carrying out a customer satisfaction study on behalf of Brieffacts Ltd., the purpose of the survey being to evaluate the level of customer satisfaction with the products and services provided by Brieffacts Ltd.

## The Brief

Brieffacts Ltd produce a range of products that are sold into two main market sectors:

- agents and trade outlets
- professional and business end users.

It is estimated that, from their customer base of 60,000, 80 per cent fall into the second category and it is this segment that are to be included in the sample for the customer satisfaction survey.

Brieffacts Ltd. will be supplied with the sample to be telephoned in either disc or label format. It is likely that telephone numbers will be supplied in most cases – if not they will be number searched.

The sample itself will be made up of a selection of professional and business customers, including local authorities, utilities, Government agencies, estate agents, solicitors, etc. The data to be gathered will cover the following areas:

- service used

- level of service provided by Brieffacts Ltd. staff

- clarity of invoicing and delivery documentation

- quality of product

- which agent was used most recently

- quality of service provided by agent

- quality of product provided by agent.

The majority of the questions will be closed, although it is anticipated that at least one open question will be included.

All information gathered during the call will then be entered on to disc and analysed.


## Methodology

Information gathered during the project will initially be recorded manually on to a questionnaire. All questionnaires will then be sight verified and input on to disc.

The benefits of having a two-stage approach, as opposed to inputting directly on to computer are:

- it allows 100 per cent concentration on the interview

- it creates a more personable and natural interview

- data is verified twice, once before inputting and once after

- specialists are used for both stages of the process.

All data input on to disc will again be sight verified before any analysis is carried out.

## Reporting and analysis

A daily report will be produced which will encompass the following areas:

- number of calls made

- number of completed questionnaires

- number of refusals

- call rate.

At the end of the research, a detailed report will be produced which will consist of counts of all the questions together with any cross tabulations that are required. Detailed written analysis will be given on a question-by-question basis, and a general summary will cover all the main conclusions of the campaign.

Brieffacts Ltd. currently employs 25 full-time salaried staff. In addition to this, we have over 60 trained temporary staff who are used on a project-by-project basis.

## Cost breakdown

**Set up, calling charges, data entry, reporting and analysis and management fee:**
**TOTAL (500 calls)** **£10,750**

All costs are quoted exclusive of VAT and subject to the terms and conditions of Brief Proposal Ltd. Payment terms to be agreed.

147

# A DETAILED PROPOSAL

## Introduction

Detailed Proposal Ltd. plans a customer monitor survey among their business and professional customers. Details of 60,000 customers are held on a database, some 80 per cent of which are thought to be from this target group.

This document seeks to explain how we would approach a study of this nature and take certain assumptions with sample design and timing. Such matters are clearly open for discussion should we be awarded the project.

## The sample

The customer database should be the main source of the sample. However, customer monitor surveys can sometimes be accused of working within a vacuum. This is because someone generally becomes a customer of an organisation if at one time, if not currently, they are satisfied that what they will be receiving (in terms of product or service) will generally be in line with their expectations. Having taken the decision to buy at some point, they will have been *de facto*, more satisfied than those who could have, but did not.

The people who are ignored by this process are therefore lapsed customers, competitor customers or non-customers of some other kind. Research among existing customers can therefore only address their needs. The needs of lapsed and/or competitor customers may have entirely different views and needs.

While it is true that customer satisfaction research is, by definition, a measurement of (current) users or buyers, its purpose is generally to retain or increase the customer base. In the latter case, it is our view that lapsed or non-customers should always be addressed.

The reason why lapsed or non-customers are neglected is frequently for reasons of practicality. Rarely is lapsing an action which is recorded. Organisations which have never been customers but could be, are difficult to find systematically.

For the meantime, we understand that 80 per cent of the customer database are customers from the professional and business sectors.

The first is a quota of particular groups to ensure the sample is representative. In other words, if 20 per cent of the customer database comprises Local Authorities, then 20 per cent of the sample should also. Provided the sample is selected randomly then the eventual sample should naturally fall out this way. However, careful sample management is necessary to ensure that this is the case, since the required number of interviews can quickly be achieved by calling 'easier to reach' respondents, rather than those who are harder to make contact with and perhaps need several call-back attempts. Typically, personnel in larger organisations and more senior personnel tend to be harder to reach. A simple quota can avoid a potential source of bias.

The second type of quota is set in order to yield sufficient numbers of interviews with particular groups or concerns. Thus, if 5 per cent of the customer base are Surveyors in private practices and the total sample for the study was

149

chosen to be 500, then only 25 Surveyors would be interviewed. Such a sample is too small to enable meaningful comparative results. It is common therefore to set a quota of a minimum number of interviews.

In order to yield results which are representative of the total customer base, two sets of data would need to be produced. The first would be a weighted set which re-sorted the sub-sample sizes to their true incidence across the database. The second would be unweighted, to look at each of the sub-samples individually.

The third type of quota is one which is based upon information which can be yielded only from the interview, not from the database. If, for example, Detailed Proposal Ltd. wished to speak to sufficient numbers of people who had contacted the company by fax, yet this information was not available on the database, then a quota may be set for this. However, accurate costing of such a quota is impossible until at least part of the fieldwork is complete, since the incidence will not be known until this point.

It is important that a sufficient contact sample exists for each quota cell and that the quota matrix is not elaborate, since this will have a major bearing on the project costs.

## Sample preparation

We are assuming that the customer database is available as a computer record.

We are able to select a sample from a diskette of the database, should this be available – we are registered with the Data Protection Registrar for this purpose. This avoids duplicated labour and means that other information (perhaps sales ordering history) can be loaded on to the sample datafile and used for subsequent cross analysis.

## The questionnaire

We have assumed that the interview length will average 15 minutes. Since the research is required to measure satisfaction across a number of dimensions, we would not recommend the use of open-ended questions since these tend to produce considerable rates of error (particularly for attitudinal-type questions). We have, however, allowed for 2 to 3 such questions in our costing.

We would suggest, regardless of our involvement in its design that the questionnaire be piloted in 'real time' prior to release to fieldwork proper. This would involve achieving six interviews and holding an informal de-brief to establish whether any slight re-wording is appropriate.

## The research method

All interviews will be conducted by telephone from a central location.

The questionnaires will be administered using Computer Assisted Telephone Interviewing (CATI) equipment. This facility enables the questionnaire to flow automatically according to the answers given by each respondent and handles rotations and text substitution routines automatically. CATI also prevents logic errors which are inevitable when a questionnaire is administered on paper.

The sample will be controlled using a Telephone Number

Management System (TNMS). This handles call-back routines, appointments, reasons for non-response etc., and is of great value in maximising response rates.

Up to four attempts will be made to secure an interview.

All interviewers are given a thorough training, regardless of claimed experience in other companies. All are specifically trained in business-to-business interviewing. Call monitoring is also used to monitor interviewer quality.

Other fieldwork quality control standards will exceed the minimum laid down by the Interviewer Quality Control Scheme (IQCS), of which we are a member. Membership of the scheme is dependent upon a successful annual inspection.

## Reporting

In customer monitor research, it is important to establish not just how individual services or departments perform, but how important each of these is in affecting satisfaction overall. In this way, an organisation can set priorities for action by concentrating on those areas which will impact satisfaction most. Multiple regression is the best method available to determine this and we have considerable expertise in this area. However, this form of analysis can be quite time consuming and we have therefore included it as an option.

If it is planned to repeat the study at some point in the future, then a regression approach would be particularly useful. This is because customer expectations are a moving target. What is less important in one year, may appear more so the next. This method will ensure that such a trend can be identified.

152

This analysis may also be used to generate a scoring system against which to set goals and measure relative performance. The process works by asking respondents to rate the performance (delivery) of a particular aspect of the service. Different points are allocated to each, based upon its importance, as measured by the regression, and its 'delivery' based upon the performance rating. In this way, more points can be gained or lost depending upon how well each aspect is delivered. Such a process of data reduction can simplify the results, making them more easily assimilated, thus improving the value of the study across the organisation.

We will provide two copies of the data tables. In addition, up to 30 summary charts will be produced to our specification in graphical format.

Plotted colour acetates are available should these be required for a presentation, at additional cost.

### Schedule

The following schedule appears realistic:

| | |
|---|---|
| Study commission | 25.05.94 |
| Agreement of first draft of questionnaire | 27.05.94 |
| Final draft | 30.05.94 |
| Questionnaire pilot | 05.06.94 |
| Sampling & CATI set-up | 08.06.94 |
| Fieldwork commences | 10.06.94 |
| Fieldwork ends | 26.06.94 |

153

| Coding & data preparation | 30.06.94 |
| Data tables | 03.03.94 |
| Charts & regression analysis | 07.07.94 |

## Fees

Our fees are subject to agreement of final questionnaire, sample structure and our terms of business. These call for settlement of 50 per cent of the survey value to be payable within 30 days of commission and the balance within 30 days of receipt of final tables and charts.

For 500 interviews including:

– Questionnaire design assistance

– CATI set-up

– Sampling

– Fieldwork

– Coding & data preparation

– Analysis (1 chart per question)

– Charts

The cost will be £11,950.00 plus VAT @ 17.5 per cent of £2,091.25, making a total of £14,041.25.

## Regression analysis

This option will incur an additional fee of £1,200 plus VAT.

## Our experience

Detailed Proposal Ltd. provides a range of qualitative and quantitative research services to business and government agencies.

The company concentrates on building a long-term relationship with its clients, believing that our contribution increases the more we understand a client's business.

Research is conducted within the UK, Europe and frequently beyond.

The company has established a reputation for premium quality telephone research. At the core of the company is a 25-station telephone centre equipped with CATI and full remote listening and VDU monitoring facilities.

Other areas of particular expertise are in technology products and financial services.

We have conducted many studies with professional groups including estate agents, solicitors, architects and construction companies.

155

# 9

# Using research to grow
# your business

## Introduction

**A**s research becomes more strategic in its contribution to companies the role of the researcher will become more important. The independent analyst can make an effective, positive and additional contribution to decision making using market knowledge, analytical experience and a clearer understanding of competitive market forces. The researcher will therefore become more effective than a communications strategist or planner. He or she will fulfil the role of corporate planner for the smaller company and strategic market analyst in the larger company. But the contribution the researcher will make will be more fundamental in creating a market-led strategy than a communications planner, as it will relate much more to the needs of the market than to creative themes designed to attract the market's attention irrespective of their needs.

Companies will want to ensure that they perform profitably in more competitive markets. Market assumptions will become less reliable than using hard market data to understand, evaluate and monitor the implementation of the sales and marketing methods required.

Every manager needs to review the role for research within the company and gain management agreement and commitment on how it can be used effectively. The most effective roles which can help companies devise the best methods to expand business are to make the research and information function central to the decision-making process and to use better data in all management meetings than is descriptive of just the sales analysis.

It is important to develop systems which are central to the whole running of the company and which input and output both internal and external data. This data needs to devise which sales, marketing and communications methods are required, which are effective and which need to have more resources allocated to help increase sales.

157

A manager cannot take the wrong decisions if he/she sets up systems which regularly provide key facts which help him/her to identify whether the sales and marketing process is progressing successfully. Brand share data will provide the statistics on how well sales are being achieved competitively. If collected in a detailed analysis this can help to establish which product categories should be developed or stimulated through promotional support to counter competitive threat.

Developing customer data and defining the user and buyer characteristics, buying habits and the nature of the customer needs within the total market will provide the key information on how to anticipate, respond to and sell to defined customer needs. An important part of this is to establish, understand and interpret the language of your customers as it will help to confirm your company's competitive unique selling points. Once these have been defined, all sales, marketing and communications methods can reflect these unique selling points and emphasise the benefits of your products and services competitively.

Once the target market is defined and the customer trends realised, it is important to segment the customers into categories which make the sales and marketing effort cost effective in its delivery. This is essential for growing the business as each market segment requires a different approach for all sales and marketing techniques. These segments also relate to how new products and services can be developed for the sub-groups that exist within the customer base. What is important for a manager is to analyse the segments clearly and understand how the trends and needs differ within each segment. Computer techniques to define the factors and clusters that exist relating the segments with lifestyles and classification characteristics will improve the market analysis and provide the manager with targets which will respond more specifically to customer-focused sales and marketing methods. Creating your own 'map' of your market and how the segments map in conjunction with the segments' trends and lifestyles, provides the best way of measuring your sales and marketing methods in the market.

Data which has been collected and analysed well also needs to be presented and reported with relevance. The data needs to address the sales and marketing problems, competitive positioning and the company's internal political issues, which must be considered useful information. What is also important is that whatever data is collected generates clear recommendations, ideas or issues that contribute to management thinking, idea generation and strategic planning. This ensures that the information that is collected is used, and its use makes a significant contribution to business planning.

When developing research programmes it is important to create a positive and constructive business relationship with the research supplier. Use of the research supplier to prove or disprove an internal political issue such as getting work done more efficiently externally than internal resources can provide, is not a sensible or profitable use of management time. Equally if the research supplier is expected to perform without laying out the parameters in which it can support your company, it is not a good investment in using market specialists. Provide the research supplier with clear and well thought out information and they will be effective in responding to you in the same way

159

## CASE STUDY

### Publishers – using research to grow their business

Companies that have benefited from using research to grow their businesses are those which have planned the research effectively. For example, publishers which have used research to take their decisions have said that a number of benefits have been realised:

- understanding their share of the market
- knowing their penetration in the different segments of the market
- identifying where their sales have been effective and where further support is required to increase sales
- better targeting to current and potential customers to communicate product and service benefits
- more realistic budgeting which has related to estimating sales and allocating the right amount of resources to increase sales.

Research for these companies has become an effective planning, monitoring and on-going decision-making tool, central to the whole process of customer-led decision making.

# Research for the future

The company of the 1990s will be one that has a good marketing information system. The management of the company will want to use information to monitor customer care and how well customers are satisfied. Data will become more significant as it will be used to prove to customers how satisfied other customers are with the style and delivery of customer service. The managers will also want to see their market shares, to check competitive sales activity and have sufficient information which indicates whether success is continuing or changing.

A user and attitude survey and an awareness and attitude survey will help to develop trend data. This trend data will monitor the customers' attitudes to your products and promotions planning. Reviewing it will influence the decisions you take as a result, by improving customer targeting or developing better promotional copy, or redesigning products or services which correspond to the changing consumer demand.

Research provides the means of getting a clear understanding of the market and the focus of market needs. It provides the mechanism for feedback and monitoring management decisions and their effectiveness.

# Conclusion

As the role of the sales force changes, so the crucial importance of research in focusing and prioritising sales actions increases. Since the mid-1980s the sales task increasingly is to prove to chosen customers that your products or services will meet their commercial requirement better than those of your competitors. Thus the sales function must be concerned with helping achieve customers' key objectives, be they profit, growth or market share. Nowadays the sales force is concerned with understanding the customer's financial pressures, industry, processes, customers and markets, and his internal procedures and policies. As a consequence, the sales person must have not only up-to-date quantitative information on all these customer aspects, but most importantly there must be qualitative assessment of how the customer views judges and values the sales proposition compared with all the competitive offerings. Without regular up-to-date research on all these aspects, the sales force will be at a severe disadvantage to their competitors and customers. Denied these vital pieces of information, the sales person is like a fully equipped infantryman without ammunition. No bullets – no bullseyes!

161

Research defines who to sell your product to in a way which the target customers relate to, through their understanding of how the product or service meets their needs, provided it is marketed in a consumer-friendly manner.

Using research to grow your business depends on the more proactive manager recognising that his/her company needs a 'culture' of using information in this way. Where research becomes effective in increasing sales is in guiding managers to change their preconceptions and previous decisions and updating them in line with changing consumer needs.

Growing the business may present its complexities and uncertainties. Using market research to grow the business does not just reduce the risk, it helps management to confirm that their decisions have a competitive edge and will result in achieving new sales and eventually, committed customers. Market research is only effective if it is actioned; actioning it produces tangible benefits to the running and development of the business.

# Appendix I
# Questionnaire design

■

## INTRODUCTION

One of the most complex aspects of carrying out market research is the development and construction of questionnaires for survey research. Many people think that the process of asking questions is easy, but in reality it is a skill that has to be learnt very carefully, otherwise the information that is collected may be worthless. Those that have little skill at designing questionnaires also find that when they try it the design of the questions is limited, and they attribute the unhelpful data to the research rather than the bad phraseology of the questions. Questionnaire design has to produce a document which is:

- easy to administer, read out or fill in by both an interviewer and an informant

- constructed in a way that answers the research hypothesis or research problem, but also has the capability to identify new issues

- easy to analyse and can provide all the characteristics of the informant being interviewed.

## TECHNIQUES FOR DESIGNING QUESTIONNAIRES

The key point to remember about questionnaire design is to make the interview possible for all those using the document. It has to have the following characteristics:

163

- **A logical sequence.** This is important as the questions must follow on logically. If they do, the interviewer will establish and maintain a rapport and collect the data required without interruptions caused by inappropriate construction or repetitive questions. Intrusive questions are more likely to be answered if they are inserted into the sequence once the rapport has been established and built.

- **Good wording.** The successful questions or the questions that ensure that a survey is successful are those that are short, specific, clear and unambiguous. Try to help the informant by specifying clearly what you want to evaluate and where possible show examples or illustrations with detailed descriptions.

164

- **Write a clear layout.** A questionnaire is a working document. A question, the possible list of answers precoded on the questionnaire, the instructions to the interviewers, and the analysis instructions all have to be clear so that the interviewer does not get confused or reads out the wrong words. Distinguish between all of these very carefully. Interviewers' instructions should be in capitals and underlined. Hand-out cards and visual prompts should be large enough to be read by the informants with poor sight. If the next question to be asked depends on the answer to the current question, routing and 'slip' instructions should be printed alongside the relevant answers clearly to help the logical sequence.

- **A reasonable length.** A street or doorstep interview should not last more than ten minutes. An in-home interview should be no more than one hour. A shop or trade interview or business-to-business interview should not last more than 45 minutes.

A questionnaire which is of reasonable length is one which is sufficiently long to collect the required information. It is one which is interesting to the informant and it should be able to help the informant to learn about their attitude to the subject or issue being researched.

Good questions depend on good design, but this can vary when behaviour and attitudes have to be measured and monitored. The essential part of monitoring behaviour is to obtain an accurate recall of what a person did. The effective way of doing this is to ask a series of questions about recent events that the informant might relate to – 'when did you last look at, buy or talk to. . .?'

165

Attitudes, opinions and images are generally measured by developing scales. Verbal scales are more easily understood than numerical scales or making a rating which takes a score out of ten. There are also different options for scales:

- **Unipolar scales.** A five-point scale from 'Good' to 'Not Very Good'
- **Bipolar scales.** A five-point scale from 'Very Good' to 'Very Bad'
- **Rating scales based on getting some type of agreement to statements.** 'Agree Strongly, Agree, Neither Agree nor Disagree, Disagree and Disagree Strongly' provides this analysis.
- **Smiley scales are used for children.**

## CONCLUDING THE INTERVIEW

Classification data is needed to finish the interview effectively. There are essentially three reasons for this:

- to ensure the right person is collected for the sample being researched

- to validate the interview in quality control procedures as laid down in the Codes of Conduct of the survey research sector

- to collect factors which can be used as variables for analysis.

What is increasingly important about classification data is that it must be used to develop more information on the habits and lifestyle of the informants. This is used to analyse and explain the answers given to the rest of the questionnaire.

166

## CONCLUSION

A good questionnaire is one which examines the habits, awareness, attitudes and needs of an informant and how all of these relate. In this way consumer behaviour can be analysed, understood and even simulated to predict how it could change. Questionnaire design is an art and not a science, and therefore it depends on an individual's creative powers to get it right.

# Appendix II
# Computer analyses

■

**D**ata analysis has an important function in making information not just actionable but effective for developing conclusions and recommendations from the research. The analysis may assist the data user to interpret and understand aspects of the data which may not have originally been realised. In fact, poor data anlaysis may cause the research to appear to be useless, and so each data set that is developed has to be checked carefully.

167

The basic analysis technique as in Figure 1 is to look at the results of each question, analysed by the classification data – age, sex and social class, type of company, number of employ-

**Figure 1 Example of a basic question analysis**

*Q1:* Do you know the answer to this question?
*Base:* All who were asked the question

| | | Age | | | Region | |
|---|---|---|---|---|---|---|
| | *Total* | *18–34* | *35–44* | *45–65* | *North* | *South* |
| **TOTAL** | 300 100% | 100 100% | 150 100% | 50 100% | 98 100% | 202 100% |
| **YES** | 266 83% | 92 92% | 142 95% | 42 84% | 85 86% | 181 90% |
| **NO** | 24 12% | 8 8% | 8 5% | 8 16% | 12 12% | 12 6% |
| **Refused** | 10 5% | – | – | – | 1 1% | 9 9% |

**Figure 2  Example of an analysis with statistics**

|  | Total | Male | Female |
|---|---|---|---|
| **Total** | 1300 | 649 | 651 |
| **Agree Strongly (+2)** | 128<br>10% | 66<br>10% | 62<br>10% |
| **Agree (+1)** | 535<br>41% | 283<br>44% | 252<br>39% |
| **Neither Agree nor Disagree (0)** | 312<br>24% | 136<br>21% | 176<br>27% |
| **Disagree (-1)** | 98<br>8% | 45<br>7% | 53<br>8% |
| **Disagree Strongly (-2)** | 14<br>1% | 3<br>– | 11<br>2% |
| **Don't Know** | 213<br>16% | 116<br>18% | 97<br>15% |
| **Mean Score** | 0.61 | 0.68 | 0.54 |
| **STD DEV** | 0.86 | 0.82 | 0.88 |
| **STD ERR** | 0.03 | 0.04 | 0.04 |

ees and turnover. This provides the initial 'picture in the frame of the movie' and quickly indicates which aspect of the information is interesting, which is useful and which can be interpreted for further implications. Often, when the interpretation is made, it is realised that further analysis is required. One question might have to be cross analysed with another question to identify the strength of opinion of one of the key groups that have been classified. Key groups may need to be regrouped into different classifications to look at the significance of the results within the original groups, as the initial classification may have been too general.

Some surveys also indicate attitude statements which require statistical measures in the tables. Usually the respondents in the survey have been asked to say how much they agree or disagree with a particular statement. The computer allocates a score to the answers, +2 for Agree Strongly to −2 for Disagree Strongly. Multiplying the number of respondents by each score enables the software to give the following measures:

- a mean score – an average within the sub-groups
- a standard deviation – a measure of the average deviation of the sample from the mean
- a standard error of the mean – an estimate of the standard deviation of the population from which a sample is drawn.

The most important factor in setting computer analyses is to think about the analysis you will need before designing the questionnaire. But sometimes this does not work out. I completed a survey a few years ago interviewing buyers in bookshops that did not work out when we ran the computer analysis. 1,000 people had been interviewed, 600 of whom had been buyers and 400 had been non-buyers. The computer analysis provided data which divided into too many small groups to make it an analysis which could provide good data. The solution to the problem was to get someone to read all of the 1,000 questionnaires and draw up an analysis of how the questionnaires had been answered and where certain 'language' indicated the type of behaviour and attitude of the informant affected the buying pattern. The analysis of this was computed and there was a clear distinction in the interpretation of the data analysis between the different socio-economic groups in the survey.

Where computer tabulations become more complex is in the

process of turning data into information, supplemented by additional analysis tools. Statistical techniques exist which examine many variables simultaneously. This is helpful for examining interrelationships within the original data analysed on a basic computer tabulation. These are the techniques for multivariate analysis and they are used for market segmentation, preference analysis, forecasting and product definition.

The two types of analysis used to segment markets are factor analysis and cluster analysis. Factor analysis examines the responses to a battery of attitude statements. It groups those questions which have been answered in a similar way. The resultant factors are then analysed by a cluster analysis which groups the respondents who answer particular questions in the same way.

The techniques for preference analysis depends on the requirement of the researcher. 'Round Robin' analysis can be used to indicate if there are differences between preference ratings if the informant has rated a number of products. Conjoint analysis is used to identify whether package style is more important than the size and which is preferred.

Forecasting techniques include multiple regression and time series analysis. Product mapping is achieved by correspondence analysis and multi-dimensional scaling. Correspondence analysis is a technique which produces maps which can be easily interpreted and show which products are preferred in a similar manner.

A manager reading this book will need to know what technique is required and when to apply it. He or she will not need to understand complex programming aspects of the computer analysis as he/she will be more interested in the results of using it. What is important is to know what analysis is required when planning the survey.

# Glossary

■

It is always of concern to management that the advertising, research and computer sectors are full of jargon. You have to be in the 'knowledge' to be able to use this jargon and if used incorrectly it can almost contribute to you becoming alienated and not accepted among the users of the specialist techniques. Therefore, I felt it worthwhile to list out the key research jargon and to identify the usefulness of the techniques described. This glossary, therefore, is the key checklist of everything a manager must know to use and perform with research effectively.

### Attitude statements

A psychological concept designed to evaluate and investigate values, beliefs and motives for different forms of behaviour.

Developing statements to describe your company and its products and services compared with those of your competitors provides the means of creating a 'control', asking consumer opinion as to whether they agree or disagree with the attitudes and, in time, monitoring the changes.

### Cluster analysis

A technique of multivariate analysis which identifies groups of individuals that are similar and different from each other. It is a way of establishing whether a group of people have similar attitudes or characteristics which helps to define or confirm sub-segments of a market.

It is an important technique for defining which types of product suit different types of consumer and also establishing whether communications can be developed for specific market segments.

## Conjoint analysis

A method of evaluating consumer preferences among product concepts which vary in respect of several attributes, based on asking people to rank which they most and least prefer.

Using this analysis helps to develop data on how certain types of customer have a preference for purchasing and using certain typest of product. It will therefore define what is the ideal product for customers because of how well the product meets their needs.

## Demographics

Sex, age and social grade are the key parts of the classification data in research and comprise the demographics of the market being researched.

173

It is vital for defining a market initially to know who are the current and potential customers. It has to become the basic 'benchmark' data on which psychographic analyses are developed and created.

## Desk research

It is based on the use of secondary data, collecting all published and existing information that is relevant to the company's markets and products. Collection of this information is important in understanding markets and to help to design survey research, ensuring that a survey does not collect data that already exists.

## Family life cycles

Stages in the development of families – young single people and young couples, the early stage; couples with children at home, the mid-life stage; and older people without children, the late stage.

## Forecasting

Estimating the expected quantity of probability of an event in the future. It may also be a prediction mode using a mathematical model, or from an extrapolation of current trends.

This is important as a technique in a defined market which can be tracked by monitoring key facts, habits and activities of the market which has been classified. It is particularly useful as a way of analysing products and product performances if product design or formulation is changed to alter the market or sales in the market.

### Geodemographics

A method of classifying households based on multivariate analysis of data from the Census of Population. The practical application of geodemographic classifications generally depends on computer matching addresses to enumerate districts by means of the post-code.

The application of geodemographics is useful for direct marketing, retail planning or developing promotions and specific marketing activities for monitoring markets or ethnic groups.

### Image statements

Consumers' perceptions or impressions of your company, product or service expressed in a clear statement.

These are used to establish how close to or far away your ideas, concepts and strategies are from consumer needs.

### Market mapping

A 'map' which shows the relative positions of the products in the market, consumers or consumer characteristics. It is the most effective method for summarising the findings of attitude research.

There are two applications for market mapping. The first is literally to draw up the structure of the market and to add to the map the facts about each level of the market – the volume of sales, the classification of the customer types, etc. It is particularly good for understanding a market more clearly.

The second is to use the analysis of survey research and to plot on a map the relationship between the defined customer types and the way in which attitudes are described or product attributes are rated. It is good for developing a product or communications strategy in sophisticated markets where it is important to develop strategies to respond to consumers' changing and demanding needs to counter competitive threats.

## Market segmentation

Using classifications or market facts to divide a market into the characteristics of the product or service, user and buyer in the market, type or size of company.

A central and very important marketing technique, market segmentation is a key tool to making research useful to grow business. It allows customer types and their different needs to be analysed, interpreted and monitored effectively. It assists in understanding how the market divides and how customers behave in different ways with different needs.

## Marketing information system

All the information available to management, together with the hardware for its storage, processing and retrieval. Market intelligence, reports from all departments and market research are all part of this system.

Creating, using and monitoring such a system is important for making the organisation customer-oriented.

## Modelling

A model is a summary of observations, including mathematical models. It is a way of 'imitating' or 'copying' the market forces and testing out changes in a market and then observing the effects that result.

It is a technique which is particularly effective in product and service research. It helps to anticipate market changes and move quickly once the effects of competitors' activity are re-analysed in the model.

## Multivariate techniques

Multivariate techniques are those which examine the relationships among a number of variables. They include analysis of variance, multi-regression, factor and principal component analysis, cluster analysis and discriminant analysis.

Application of these techniques to survey analysis provides the manager with the opportunity to advance product and communications planning. It helps to translate the methods of marketing into the language and behaviour of consumers.

## Paired comparison test

A test to compare two products or samples with the purpose of getting a user or buyer to discriminate between them or identify changes or improvements.

It is an important way of developing data to identify users' and buyers' attitudes to competitors' products and establish consumers' perceived benefits of your own.

## Psychographic analysis

A segmentation application which classifies people into groups based on their behaviour or attitudes.

It is becoming more and more important as a technique as it helps to classify and group the customers in a market, reflecting their needs in the context of their preferences and buying habits. It helps to make communications more direct and relevant and to make market analysis more realistic in the context of getting to know the customer.

## Regression analysis

A statistical method of calculating an equation which is applied to a set of bivariate or multivariate observations.

It is a useful technique for analysing different market segments to identify whether any of the sub-groups of customer have any similarities in behaviour, attitudes or preferences.

### Sample

A representation of the whole whose purpose is to be able to investigate the characteristics of the population. It is comprised of parts or sub-sets of the population being researched. Survey research depends on getting this right as a survey completed with the wrong type of population is worthless.

### Sampling

The technique for selecting a sample. It depends on setting up a sampling frame and identifying sampling units which comprise a population.

Survey research is only successful if this is completed well.

### Trade-off models

A technique which is used to discover the most attractive combination of attributes for a product or service by the respondent expressing a preference for one or other alternative.

An important technique for understanding clearly why people buy and how they evaluate whether the product or service that is offered corresponds with their needs and the way in which they decide on making the purchase.

# Index

■

181